CRISIS CASH MANAGEMENT

"Saving your business when cash is running out"

JIM ROHR

ISBN: 1-4392-6252-7
ISBN-13: 9781439262528

Library of Congress Control Number: 2009910901

Disclaimer: Notice is hereby given to the reader of this publication that James A. [illegible] and any assigned agents, shall assume no liability whatsoever, expressed or implied under any theory of law, for the reader's interpretation, application or use of these [illegible] contained [illegible]. It is highly recommended [illegible] professional financial assistance [illegible] money [illegible] results of [illegible] is considered to be used [illegible] should be read in conjunction with and [illegible] by the reader [illegible] experience [illegible] professional assistance [illegible] and [illegible] by the reader.

DEDICATION:

This humble work is dedicated to our loving God, who in Him all things are possible in the name of his loving son, Jesus Christ.

Now that God is on our side...
Let's go save your business from this cash crisis.

TABLE OF CONTENTS

TABLE OF CONTENTS

PREFACE

This book titled "**Crisis Cash Management**" (CCM) is a no nonsense, information resource and "how to" guide for any business in a cash crisis. This Guide teaches the critical art and skills of **crisis cash flow management**...a term I created to describe management of the business when the world is closing in due to cash issues. Call it a "crisis situation" or a whatever you like. **The bottom line is the business is in trouble and needs to bail itself out.** CCM is based on sound principals and "trial by fire" methodologies. It includes practical advice, roles and responsibilities, cash control, cash flow knowledge and hundreds of experienced based cash recovery knowledge lessons you can apply in your business right now...today. ***You don't have a minute to loose.***

"Cash is definitely King" in personal and business finance. Only cash can pay for debts of a business...not inventory, good will or high brow branding. It's true that most disciplined Managers can operate a business under favorable cash conditions. It's when times are tough that Crisis Cash Management (CCM) can help small and medium sized business owners and managers survive a daily "make it or break it" cash crisis.

Crisis Cash Management is not about managing cash in banks to achieve optimum rates of return, nor is it about dividends, macro conditions, or investing cash. Instead, CCM helps Managers and Owners take control of business cash and create cash position certainty and positive cash flow. You will use a very granular time cycle for reporting, analysis and follow up. You will use a "rolling wave of knowledge" approach to keep the information accurate and current. This book will help you produce all the information needed and will manage the recovery of the business during the crisis and beyond.

Crisis Cash Flow Management skills elude many owners and managers. Crisis Cash Management is just not a routine condition for most Managers....but it must be understood if the company is going to survive. "Seat of the pants" cash management methods are not sufficient to recover a declining cash condition.

Even a bad cash management system works when enough cash is coming in.

Crisis Cash Management is not taught in business schools...even though all Business Majors receive well focused training on the subject. What they don't teach is Crisis Cash Flow Management, a unique set of skills akin to that of a survivalist in the woods...making do with what they have, finding food wherever it lies. Crisis Cash Management is an "acquired skill"...developed in battle and tested under fire.

Either you acquire the skills or you don't. If you do, the business survives. If not, well...someone else will be buying your assets for nickels on the dollar.

Business depressed financial conditions coupled with global declining markets are forcing even experienced managers to address and become experts in Crisis Cash Management for the first time. For those brave few, it's time to acquire Crisis Cash Management as a new core competency and as a way of business life. This rigid discipline of perfect cash flow management is making companies agile, leaner and in the process, survivors. What company would not want to be more agile and leaner during turbulent times?

When cash flow margins are declining or negative, managers under fire don't need long dissertations on cash flow theory or advance cash management techniques. They need a "basic guide". One which provides the key skills and advice for ***repetitive and sustainable cash and cash flow management techniques...especially under poor economic market conditions and when cash is just plain absent, regardless of reason***. "Crisis Cash Flow Management" answers these needs with heavy emphasis on business survival during negative cash flow conditions or when the business is just losing control of cash flow.

Is your company in a cash crisis? If it is, corporate wealth is decreasing. If the cash condition is acute...the very survival of the businesses is in jeopardy.

Organization of this Guide

This Guide is divided into two (2) parts:

Part 1: Crisis Cash Management - Information and Opinions
Part 2: Crisis Cash Management Plan – Template

Please read Part 1 first to gain concepts and suggestions that will support Part 2, Plan Development and Plan Performance. You have several difficult things to accomplish quickly to gain control of your cash, so try to read Part 1 in one reading. Then read Part 2 in one reading if possible before jumping in.

You should be able to read this complete book in about ten hours at 50 WPM average speed. However, implementing the information in this Guide can and will take several days.

For some companies, it might take only a day or two to achieve cash certainty and full process control. If that reference does not describe your company, then it may take days of number crunching and some guess work to perform just a few steps. This is almost always true when cash based information is scattered, missing, or off site. Either way, it WILL become accurate and well structured for assimilation and analysis.

Your specific success depends greatly on the level of effort applied by all stakeholders.

Good luck, read on, and get ready to go to work....your business might just depend on it.

PART I

Crisis Cash Management – Information and Opinions

Problem Statements

I can group two classes of companies, both with basically the same need. Each comes from two distinctly different business problems.

1. **This Guide shows business stakeholders how to survive when cash is declining or absent...and even excel when others are failing.** So this Guide is for those companies who have found themselves in a "cash crisis" and need help dealing with the conditions. Some companies manage cash resources better than others...even in a cash crisis. Some lack the discipline to manage cash in a very finite manner when cash is absent or missing, regardless of reason.
2. **This Guide is for all those companies who just wake up one day and find themselves in a cash crisis...regardless of reason.** Does anyone disagree that today's marketplace is in "decline" in several sectors? If your company is in the decline due to external conditions, your sales have dropped substantially. Firms I talk to are reporting a loss of sales by as much as 50% compared to previous levels of economic normalcy and traditional market growth. On the upside, some businesses are surviving and even growing using very creative recovery means. On the down side, other business owners are watching their hard earned assets sold off to pay for past routine obligations. Still other owners watch as their principal, home and personal assets are sold off because they signed for the business credit they received some years back. As of this writing, it doesn't look good for most businesses selling "nice to have" and "should have' products and services. Better to be selling "must have" items.

Compounding both problem classes, taxation rates are likely to climb even higher as State and Government entities attempt to recapture lost operating tax revenue from a declining tax base or need your money to finance the future. Regulations are coming in books that need specialists just to interpret. For businesses who remain standing, expect a long and very bumpy ride back to prosperity as taxation and regulation increase.

Key Guide Objectives

My first and most important objective for you dear reader is I want you to understand that the information, advice and lessons contained in this essential Guide can be applied almost immediately to your business. The time to act is right NOW...especially if cash flow is declining or negative. Don't hesitate another minute. Time is definitely not on your side and in fact, **time is actually working against your success**....and I will show you why later on.

The second key objective of this Guide, is to teach the business owner, operating manager or key stakeholders the critical art and skills of **"crisis cash management".**

Let's start this important journey by defining some goals for effective Crisis Cash Management. We need to know when we have arrived as these skills will be needed over the entire life of the business.

The principal goals of crisis cash management are:

1. To understand the **fundamental axioms of cash management and principals of making and handling money during a declining cash business**
2. Learn the **"Critical Success Factors"** of effective crisis cash management
3. Learn how to **record cash** in such a way as to **increase cash knowledge and thus improve cash position confidence**
4. Learn how to plan for and support **maximized cash inflow**
5. Learn how to **establish cash priorities**
6. Learn how to time and negotiate payments for current and long term **business obligations**
7. Learn how to **identify, monitor and control cash risk**
8. Learn how to establish **roles, responsibilities and accountability** that ensure success...and in some cases even business survival.

Lot's of learning. By applying the lessons in this Guide, (and those discovered through practice and independent research), a prudent Manager can **"master business cash flow...under almost any cash condition".**

By now you are wondering who else should read this. Well here is one answer.

Guide and Plan Distribution Recommendations

It's up to you to decide how you want this information distributed, however, I recommend that you buy a copy of this book for each "Core Team" member you select. That would be about six copies. At a minimum, I recommend that you have a least three copies available for people to refer to as the initiative comes together and unfolds. Trust me, you will buy the other three.

Let's talk about distribution. Parts of this Guide, (and the Plan created in Part 2), should be distributed within the enterprise in three principal ways:

Part 1 and 2 – Owner, Senior Managers with Profit and Loss Responsibility, Managers and Core Team Members.

Part 2 – Key Stakeholders and Supporting Contributors such as Business Unit Leaders, Accounting Staff, Banks, Bookkeeping and Others. Anyone you share your financial records with.

Components of Part 2 – Lower level personnel in Marketing, Sales, Purchasing, and others who spend or make money for your business. Also, I want you to consider looking outside the business to your key suppliers! Suppliers and banks can make or break your recovery plan and survival. Involve them.

I am going to amplify each of these stakeholders in far more detail later on, so relax. The important thing to take away here is:

Some need to know it all...Some need to know the Plan...and some stakeholders need only to know their portion of the Plan.

I have found it is always better to share more information when business survival is at stake. You have everything to gain and little to lose.

Basic CCM Concepts

- Cash inflow comes from all sources of inflow including sales receipts, lease payments and interest on money in your bank to name a few larger income streams.
- Cash outflow comes from spending regardless of reason.
- A "cash crisis" exists whenever the the difference between cash inflow and cash outflow ("the net cash flow margin") is negative or declining for more than two time periods in a row. I don't care if they are days, weeks or months. If you get two in a row, it's a crisis.

A negative cash flow margin occurs whenever cash outflow exceeds cash inflow to the business over a given and measurable time period.

A declining cash flow margin is just as critical as a negative one...it has just not yet turned negative.

Either way, corporate wealth is being drained away from the enterprise. This measure of loss or gain in corporate wealth is found through precise cash flow analysis. It is the "dashboard indicators" that show the progress towards predetermined cash management goals. Let's go spend some profit....what no cash?

Profits vs Cash

Its impossible to spend profit. It's easy to spend cash. Before we "jump into the deep end" as my dad used to say, we should remember the difference between cash and profit.

Important Concepts

Profits are opinions...but cash is FACT

Financial statements may show profit...yet the money (cash) in the bank may not reflect the profits declared.

You can't pay bills with money (cash) that does not exist. Therefore, we will use cash as the basis for managing the financial health of the enterprise...not profit.

If you do not learn the difference between profit, earnings and cash, your success will be derailed or significantly undermined from the get-go. "Earnings" are what a public company reports as the income for a given period. Earnings lack a relationship to the true cash flow of the company and therefore stated earnings are a weak tool to understand if the company is actually making money or loosing money. Large companies can show negative earnings for perhaps years and still be profitable. The reason for this is charges to earnings such as Depreciation. Depreciation is included in net earnings and clouds whether the firm is loosing money or not. Depreciation like other charges are a "bookkeeping charge" where no actual money (cash) is outlaid. Asset rich companies can manipulate this charge so the net result of earnings can be adjusted to suit a desired reported value. A small shop owner with limited assets cannot do this. They live in a world of cash. In contrast to earnings, cash flow analysis is a more accurate means to understand the financial performance of the enterprise.

The critical aspect of time

Valuable time is slipping by. If your company cash flow margin is declining or negative, the time is now to **"Stop Bleeding Cash".** Let me give you a visual image to accentuate the issue.

> Imagine the visual image of a patient who is losing their important and limited blood supply. In declining or negative cash flow, the patient (your business) is losing blood (cash) faster than it is taking blood (cash) in. How long this negative blood loss (financial condition) can occur is largely up to your actions to "stop the bleeding", (make new cash and slow the consumption of the liquid cash reserves available to the business). Think of cash reserves as the "blood reserve" of the patient. Both making and managing cash are dependent on each other.

What is a Business Enterprise

I believe you really do not own anything...but are stewards of God's wealth for as long as He wishes. It is up to you to do the most with what God has given you to work with.

The purpose of every business is to create value for buyers and turn a net profit. A company is a legal entity with an infrastructure, (people, processes, technology, assets), specifically designed to satisfy target customers through the efficient supply of goods, services and/or information with the net result of creating profit. Customers pay money to the business for goods, services and information. When customer payments are sufficient enough and managed correctly, excess money allows the company to stay in business and grow. A prosperous business is one where after meeting all current obligations, (payroll, taxes, debt payments, supplier payments, etc), there remains sufficient cash, ("net profits"), in the business to meet or exceed desired goals and objectives of the owner, or the stockholders.

A business as a commercial enterprise must make a profit (net cash on hand) if it is to survive long term.

If profits and demand are sufficient, decisions are made to grow the business. When profits do not exist, the business either changes so it can make a profit, or is sold off (handed off) to someone who will turn a profit, or it is dismantled for the value of its assets and it dies. There are few other options. Without cash, the business will ultimately file for legal protection.

In business, (as it is in life), there always seems to be a need for more cash, than is available. Proper cash flow management promotes an increase in corporate wealth, sustains business growth, handles routine cash outflows, records inflows and outflows with certainty and improves business financial and functional operating efficiency.

Its impossible to drive a car safely when the dash board instruments don't function and the windows are painted black.

CCM needs a working dashboard. In good times and bad, managing cash flow, (income and outflows) must be done. Managing cash flow and setting spending priorities should be an everyday business activity. Managing cash flow is essential to the health and financial stability of the company. Cash Management is therefore necessary for the allocation of a limited amount of resources, (cash reserves), in the most effective direction which propels the business forward with confidence and lowest possible risk.

If you are like most Business Managers, you started your business, (or decided to Manage one), so it would prosper, succeed and grow...even through hard times. However noble these goals are, they will be significantly challenged unless the critical skill of CCM is known and when necessary, applied. For those that do not learn this critical skill, the progression to ruin will be:

1. Suffer an incredible loss of corporate wealth for as long as cash reserves exist, or,
2. The business perishes when reserves expire and/or credit lines run out.

Both of the above is a failing of management to embrace CCM loss reversal techniques and change the business so it can prosper. No one wants to close their business unwillingly. However, to ultimately survive a cash crisis, the enterprise must perform six main cash flow functions within the time remaining of corporate life...all within the constraints of available assets, technology, processes, financial resources, regulations and personnel:

1. Form a sense of urgency and team spirit across the enterprise
2. Stop the financial bleeding from the enterprise and control expenses
3. Pump or earn new financial blood (cash) into the enterprise
4. Synchronize cash flow in and out of the enterprise
5. Monitor the vital signs of the enterprise to know if changes make a positive effect
6. Make changes in the business model to allow for more inflow than outflow which results in a net operating cash reserve

Cash flow and money axioms

Golden nuggets all.

- You (the owner, manager) are solely responsible for your current cash situation
- If you want to improve your cash situation, increase your inflow of cash, decrease your outflow of cash, or optimally both
- Your company's cash position is a direct reflection of internal and external conditions acting on your given business model
- A bad business model and value proposition cannot be cured by effective cash flow management...but it helps
- Cash received in the form of Debt is a short term solution...no matter how long the note is written for
- Avoid taking on more debt, especially to save a dying business
- Adding personal money in a declining business condition is NEVER a good idea
- A declining market, a poor business model, or both, cause net cash to decrease
- In a "cash environment", you cannot spend cash you don't have
- Hard and soft assets recorded on the books are not "liquid cash"
- A good goal for any business is to have cash reserves equal to a minimum of two years worth of net operating expenses without any income
- The larger the company, the longer they can usually survive a declining cash position...this is because of larger credit and asset resources

What will "Crisis Cash Management" do for my business?

1. Provides critical steps you can take today to stop financial cash flow "bleeding"
2. Gets control over all cash into and out of the enterprise
3. Dramatically increases an understanding of the current cash position
4. Substantially increases cash horizon certainty
5. Exposes needs to raise new cash
6. Supports payments with cash outflow certainty
7. Supports cash inflow accountability and monitors inflow risk
8. Helps plan debt reduction initiatives
9. Determines when new bills can be paid
10. Reduces pressure on existing credit lines and provides confidence to obtain more debt
11. Promotes ideas to make additional money
12. Promotes increased cash reserves for growth or unplanned fluctuations in cash flow

13. Predicts the immediate financial future of the business
14. Anticipates short-term cash needs
15. Predicts seasonal cash fluctuations through history data and advanced forecasting
16. Helps plan larger capital expenditures and expansion (e.g. equipment and inventory) purchases
17. Helps take advantage of cash discounts
18. Promotes long term strategic planning
19. Active tool to increase investment income for owners and shareholders

The Basics: Cash Flow = Cash Receipts – Cash Disbursements

Cash Receipts include any cash inflow, (money), the company receives from any source, (operations or other), including:

1. Billed Sales
2. Progress Payments
3. Customer Advances
4. Interest on Loans
5. Rent or Rental Receipts
6. Cash Sales
7. Other Receipts

Cash Disbursements include any cash out flow (payments of money) made by the company for expenses like:

1. Payroll
2. Accounts Payable
3. Taxes
4. Lease Payments
5. Retirement Payments
6. Interest Payments
7. Debt Payments
8. Other Planned and Unplanned Payments

If the result of the cash flow equation is positive and growing as compared to last period, then the company is gaining corporate wealth and alternatively, if the result of the cash flow equation is less than the last period or negative, then the company is loosing corporate wealth.

What is a "cash flow crisis?"

A cash flow crisis, (in business or personal finance), is when "there is less money (or no money) available to meet current obligations". Please note, I did not say "to meet current business opportunities"...as there are always more opportunities to spend money in a business, than available financial resources to pay for them.

In a cash crisis, what we care most about is not profit or planned disbursements as these are a mix of actual and planned events. **What we care most about in a crisis is the actual cash going into and going out of the firm.**

It should be self-evident when a company is in "critical cash mode". The signs are everywhere. Suppliers and creditors are calling wanting payment, employees are being laid off, purchases are delayed, assets are being sold off. There is no money to pay for inventory, new computers, production tools...anything.

In difficult times when cash is extremely limited, variations between inflow and outflow cause cash reserves to be consumed and used up. When cash reserves are being consumed or are absent, (including available credit), prompt steps must be taken to ensure inflow and outflow synchronize.

Cutting outflow is a first step towards recovery. If the condition is acute, steps might include delaying payments, letting employees go, selling assets and reducing overhead...to name a few. However, these are temporary "stop gap measures" and further weaken the business...yet they do buy some limited time to find a means of recovery.

Accurate Cash Flow Projections therefore become critical in times of financial trouble. The significance occurs in both the time horizons used and need for greater accuracy of cash inflows and outflows. **Differences between "projections" of cash income and outflow, and "actual" cash income and outflows are a main source of financial trouble as actual cash funds may not be available to cover planned payment events.**

A company must be able to rely on cash flow projections if longer-range cash commitments are to function and work. In terms of cash income and outflow, any variation between "projected and actual" figures results in financial instability to the degree of the variation…a negative condition that must be avoided at all cost.

Cash Management therefore is a detailed management of cash inflow, cash outflow, projections of inflow and outflow, people, responsibility, and accountability. This heightened process of cash management naturally interfaces with other cash creation efforts, cash reserve management and corporate debt management processes.

Do I need to learn this critical skill? Yes. I assume you do or the information in this Guide would not be important to you. If it is essential you learn these skills, then your business future may actually depend on it.

Do I need to make critical decisions using these skills? Yes. You will be making critical decisions that will have long term effects on your business and personal life, and the lives of your workers and suppliers. Because of this fact, it is essential that the decisions made are under the best possible conditions and use the best information available.

Can I apply this skill throughout my life? Yes. The skill is applicable to both business and personal cash management.

How fast can I apply this skill? Immediately.

I once had an internal accountant named Bill while General Manager of a leading tooling company. He would frequently say, "Knowing the number of days of corporate life remaining before your company becomes technically insolvent is a good measure of business financial direction and financial health". I could not agree with Bill more. Thanks Bill for that insight.

This simple "days of life" number measured many factors including; the degree of positive, negative or declining cash flow margin, the outflow rate, the inflow rate and on hand cash reserves, (without any remaining credit advances), to keep the business technically alive. When the number was shrinking, prudence suggested that the management team must intervene quickly to arrest declines.

This metric is akin to monitoring declining cash flow margins. **When cash flow margins are negative, managers must act immediately and decisively to arrest the condition.** Cash on hand is not an endless resource for companies. Management intervention must return the negative cash flow margin back to positive if the business is to survive. To be successful, decisive intervention must include making sweeping changes in one or more difficult areas...including layoffs. We need to be able to recognize the condition, take bold steps to arrest the causes and stop the consequences by applying CCM techniques.

Side Bar

You can estimate the # of days of corporate life remaining by dividing the current average daily outflow into the sum of all cash on hand (including liquid cash reserves).

A positive cash flow margin is the normal state of profitability, as it allows for the finance and payment of long term goals of the company...including growth. However, when cash flow margins are negative, even short term expenditures are at risk, like paying this weeks payroll or meeting other financial obligations. Without valid and realistic information the crisis condition may not even be known except empirically...or "the day the cash ran out". Therefore, the steps a Manager must take depend greatly on when in the decline spiral you recognize the crisis cash condition.

Let's look at the spiral of enterprise failure in more detail in the next section. We are about to learn that CCM is the first place to arrest a failing business.

Here is a test for when the business is in a crisis:

1. My sales are dropping this month by greater than 10%.
2. I am not absolutely positive I can pay this bill with the money we have in the bank.
3. I can't tie cash outflow to incoming revenue.
4. I am not sure what income we will have next week.
5. Our net cash flow margin dropped for 2 consecutive days
6. I can't meet current financial obligations. (Actually, it was a crisis when your margin declined before going negative.)

Enterprise failure is a vicious spiral

If there ever was a time in the enterprise's life that the organization needs to pull together in one direction, it is during a cash crisis.

True. Pulling together should be the normal operating condition, but it is my experience that large and small companies suffer from this conflict to some degree. Be aware that one of the main reasons of enterprise failure is conflicting agendas and strategies within the enterprise...all placing their own demands on the available cash resources of the enterprise. It's the managers job to align these strategies and increase inflow while controlling resource outflow.

Looking at business failure in a more generalized way, the enterprise is not converting inputs, (loans, material, people's labor, what it buys), with sufficient efficiency to generate an end value someone is willing to pay for....all at a profit, of course. To stay in business the company must satisfy buyers at prices that allow the enterprise to make money and carry on.

Whenever I see an enterprise failing, I see an enterprise where the owners were unable or simply unwilling to adjust their processes, people, technology, or offerings to satisfy the true needs of the marketplace. It is also true that some business assumptions made yesterday or 10 years back has now gone terribly wrong. I can usually find that assumption and so can you.

The main symptoms of a failing enterprise are:

- Increased internal and external drama, frustration and negative emotion
- Absent cash
- Supplier payments beyond agreed terms
- Declining sales
- Ineffective or low value conversion efficiency
- Heavy discounts to move product or services
- Loss of employees
- Sale of business units or other hard and soft assets
- Any combination of the above

Most of the above symptoms are the result of a deeper problem that shows in the cash flow equation. In a general sense, disruption is the first "tell", (using poker terms), that the enterprise is failing. Negative changes occur which lead to additional demands on remaining financial resources. The decreasing cash flow margin results in lowering cash on hand, tapping remaining credit lines, creating a need for owner loans, extending supplier credit and ultimately, firing of employees and sales of hard assets. When cash resources dry up you can expect significant delays in payment to suppliers and/or banks that provided capital, taxes go unpaid, and any other combination of conditions signifying a lack of cash.

As the cash position further declines, the company must pay for what the company needs in advance, (COD and CIA)...often well before converting them to a value that someone would pay for. Payroll is usually last to be forgone.

The hard basic fact is that when cash flow is acute, the enterprise is dying at a rate equal to the decline in cash flow...offset by the remaining cash available.

With a negative cash condition, cash and credit are draining from the enterprise. The "platform is definitely burning" and the entire enterprise is at a great risk of loss unless positive changes are made...and made very quickly. Without sufficient new cash and cash controls, the enterprise is on its way to formal bankruptcy. **The enterprise must be brought into financial control, or it will die by either a decision of management, or by an external decision of it's creditors.**

Only an infusion of capital (cash) will save the financially wounded enterprise that lacks reserves, or a means to obtain cash from selling off assets. Without it, bills go unpaid, people are fired, assets are sold off and doors close.

Difference between "Crisis Cash Flow Management" and a "Business Turn Around"

A **Business Turn Around Initiative** is much more involved than a "Crisis Cash Management Initiative". A Business Turn Around takes a much wider and longer view of the business and the marketplace. You could say that a Crisis Cash Management Initiative is a component of, (and perhaps a first step towards), a Formal Turn Around Plan.

Accurate cash position knowledge is essential in any Turn Around Plan...for without the knowledge of when the cash is coming in, when it will be available to spend, who should get it and what cash direction the company is headed in, the business is all but doomed at the start of the recovery.

Crisis Cash Management (CCM) is an immediate short range intervention initiative sustained for long term management knowledge. I like to think of Crisis Cash Management as the first plan of action a doctor in the emergency room might use to save a severely bleeding patient. Your CCM Plan must be geared to "stop bleeding cash and revive the patient long enough for the business to quickly execute a longer range and wider scope turn around initiative". The goal of CCM is to fix the immediate cause of the enterprise failure...or at least slow down the bleeding long enough to make other strategic plans.

The longer range plan could be to sell the business, execute a formal "Turn Around Plan", or implement some other "Strategic Management Initiative" designed to provide for long range business stability and ultimately growth. These other plans will likely address all phases of the business including; Marketing, Sales, Production, Distribution, Finance, Opportunities, Business Model, Corporate Wealth Release and Corporate Wealth Creation, etc.

In essence, you want your Crisis Cash Management Plan to address one thing... to reverse the conditions causing or leading to the businesses negative cash flow. Unchecked, the business will fail.

Once a declining cash flow condition is slowed, stopped, and hopefully reversed, the enterprise can focus on the underlying causes of why it is failing.

What can Business Manager's control...How about

1. Keeping God first in your life and in your business
2. Better cost forecasting
3. Adequate financial controls and collecting evidence that those controls are working
4. Making cash management a core competence
5. Adequate capitalization
6. Leveraging the right finance
7. Satisfying customers
8. Making hard choices
9. Reinventing the business to suit market conditions
10. Taking bold proactive steps
11. Empowering employees
12. Higher sales
13. Attracting more customers
14. Delegating control
15. Better supply chain management
16. Eliminating material shortages
17. Protecting key supplier/s
18. Higher inventory turns
19. Lean cash outflow including indirect costs
20. Higher profit margins
21. Paying taxes on time
22. Zero product failure
23. Protecting the business from risks
24. Providing adequate insurance for unknown risks
25. Balancing ego with reality
26. Higher standard of dedication
27. Applying advanced business tools such as ERP, Activity Based Costing, Strategic Sourcing and Target Costing

Side Bar

The list on the left is only a partial list of areas a Manager can control. It was provided to show that you can estimate, manage and control your cash flow...just as you do for all the other areas of your company.

The above list includes a host of items I would call basic "good sound management". Some mentioned are normal and routine. Others will take a lot of work to accomplish, but are necessary just the same. All maximize business performance. Which leads us to the question of when should a business be saved.

How do I know if my business enterprise is worth saving?

I would turn this important question around and ask it differently, "How much are you willing to invest in time, effort and money to turn the declining or failing business into a new business that makes a respectable profit...even in tough times?" If the answer is anything but a 110% commitment, start making plans to sell it or wind it down unless you like using up your own wealth.

If you are selling "must haves" or even "should haves", then sales outlook could be good even in tough times. If you are selling "like to haves", they better be fantastic "like to haves"... because people stop buying "like to haves" when economic times are bad.

> ***Note:*** *The exception to the above generality is those companies which cater to the extremely rich. The rich can afford "like to haves" during good and bad times...but don't kid yourself...even the rich back off these expenditures when times are tough. The rich are frugal people to begin with. That is how they maintain and grow their wealth. Just like you, the rich loose money too and lot's of it when times are bad. The rich also focus on acquiring long term money making assets during hard times. They sell when times are good and buy when times are bad. This counter cyclical strategy is how the rich get VERY RICH.*

Positive and sustained Cash Flow is a main reason why companies are bought in the first place. They make money for the owners and investors, over and over. A business which has a poor cash flow is worth far less than one with a good cash flow.

Looking at purely assets. In good times, assets in distressed companies sell for as low as twenty five cents on the dollar. In bad times you can find the same items for ten cents on the dollar because the supply is greater and buyers are less frequent. Most good used assets came from a company that bled out too much cash....maybe from a company like yours!

Don't let acquisition "sharks" pick up your years of hard work for next to nothing.

To avoid the sharks, you will need a sound and reliable cash information system. One designed to prevent the cause of a Crisis Cash Condition. That same system can inform, (or at least estimate), how much cash will be required, (before and after cash correction of course), to hold the business open and improve cash margins until market conditions improves and more cash is coming in, or changes are made to reduce outflow. At least you will have a thumbnail idea of "how high the mountain is" to profitability and under what cash flow conditions in that decision process.

If you had a good sound business performing well during good times, (like selling a needed item), then that business should have the capability of surviving hard times with proper cash controls. However, if the business was struggling under good times to stay alive, it will almost certainly fail once conditions turn negative.

The final decision is yours and so is the commitment. There is one thing to remember as you make this important and critical decision.

If you are out of cash and assets that will convert to cash, you're almost out of options.

How long will it take to see results?

It all depends on you. How quickly you see results, largely depends on how aggressive you are in properly executing the Steps defined in Part 2 of this Guide together with other advice outside the scope of this resource.

I am going to give you, at the end of this Guide in Part 2, a Crisis Cash Management Plan "Template". If you gather the information required and take immediate action to reduce outflow and increase inflow, then you will see results almost immediately. If you delay either of these actions, it will ultimately be much more painful to reach cash flow stability and finally...recovery. If you delay too long, it likely will not matter as a negative cash position cannot be sustained without additional cash infusion. Let's go back to time because that was the question.

Sure, aggressive companies can reverse a declining cash position in days. Lax companies and companies with poor managers can fumble around with the initiative for weeks and still not be able to collect or leverage the information. Still others will fail at keeping the cash flow information current so that what was once real time information...quickly digresses to a useless document of history recording the failure.

Get started today...and I do mean TODAY. Your business depends on it. Once you collect the information and put in place controls, keep them current.

Who are the stakeholders of crisis cash management?

Simple answer is **anyone who directly or indirectly receives the money distributed by the business or has control over its income...including its customers.**

Naturally, a direct group includes those stakeholders internal to the business enterprise itself. For one, your employees have have a vested and direct interest in the success of the business and its cash processes. Direct stakeholders are always most affected by your business success or failure. They are also the same people that must, (in some way), be part of the **Crisis Cash Team**...since they will be ones that execute, (and are responsible for), the long term performance of the Crisis Cash Management Plan. The **Plan Leader** will be the one who is accountable for the performance of the Plan and or the business. Direct stakeholders are a given, but you also need to consider **external stakeholders.**

External to the enterprise are stakeholders like your customers, suppliers, the tax man and others who have varying interest in the performance of the enterprise. Who else outside your organization benefits from the success or failure of the business and its flow of money?

Are not your family, your bank and the families of your employees also stakeholders...albeit external and indirect? Sure they are. They all rely on the money flow from your ongoing business success as indirect beneficiaries of your business.

How about you as owner and your stockholders. Are you not a direct stakeholder of the business and have the most invested in the performance of the business.

At a minimum, I think you can agree that both direct and in some cases indirect stakeholders deserve reliable information about how your business and actions will likely affect them...not only today, but as long as

Side Bar

Stakeholders can and will have a positive or negative effect on the inflow of cash, retaining the cash you have, and slowing the outflow of available cash. As positive evidence of results increase, internal and external stakeholder confidence will rise. This confidence adds velocity to cash recovery efforts.

the association exists. If your business fails, they will be affected, (at least in part). If your business succeeds, they also will benefit....you included.

Once your Crisis Cash Plan is designed, roles and responsibilities can be defined and stakeholders will know, (when you tell them), how they will impact the Plan and what changes they can expect.

Three Step Cash Flow "Triage"

Step 1: You save the patient, (meaning your business), by taking steps to ensure that the life blood of the company, (its' cash), is "stopped" from bleeding out (paid out) of the company.

Step 2: You maintain the position in Step 1 until you have control over all cash and a plan in place to ensure the cash position is certain, (we call it "ending cash position"). (Do it really need to be said that Step 2 needs to be accomplished in hours? Maybe a day or two...but not weeks.)

Step 3: Then, once you know your cash condition with certainty, you begin cash allocations based on a predefined priority system. From allocations, disbursements can take place with confidence. That confidence comes from cash outflows tied to cash inflows, (cash on hand), not profits or projected cash. Actual cash.

Sounds simple doesn't it. Well that depends on many Prerequisite Conditions and Critical Success Factors...not to mention the actual work of change and change management control.

Let's dive in beginning with CCM Prerequisites.

Crisis Cash Management Prerequisites

1. Authority over the business and documented authority to act (make changes) as necessary
2. Detailed information about your current cash position
3. Detailed information about all receivables
4. Detailed information about all accounts payables
5. Realistic understanding of your direct expenses
6. Realistic understanding of your indirect expenses
7. Sufficient people willing to participate and work hard in the success of the Plan
8. Realistic sales forecasts...cash that actually will come in and when
9. Owner or Senior Manager contact information for your key suppliers
10. Senior Bank Manager contact information

Side Bar

Do not wait to collect this information. If you are reading this for the first time, begin now to gather the information listed here into a single place. You will need the information outlined shortly and by gathering this now you will be working in parallel as you read on. Do not delay.

11. A visible means to keep everyone informed about their individual progress towards the goals you set
12. A means to record extraordinary expenses and their maker
13. Candid assessment of current inventory and its value by item
14. Candid assessment of hard and soft assets and their value
15. Schedule of immediate cash needs (what is due for payment right now)
16. Schedule of all current outstanding obligations (payable in less then one year)
17. Schedule of long term obligations (payable later then one year)
18. One person who will collect and pivot all information...(at least initially)

Critical Success Factors

A Critical Success Factor (CSF) is a precondition or enabler that has a high bearing on the successful outcome of any action...which in this case is the creation and execution of the Plan. Following is my list of CSF's in addition to the Prerequisites.

1. Your personal accountability for the success or failure of the cash management initiative
2. Frank and realistic assessment of your current business cash condition...this is not a time to let ego or wishful thinking enter into a logical process
3. Willingness to make bold changes in your business...including its cash processes
4. Decisive action, (at the right time), according to your predefined structured Crisis Cash Management Plan
5. Full ownership of the "process of change" and the outcome
6. Effective high leadership to define the common goals and develop consciousness within the organization sufficient to accomplish the goals set
7. Effective Team willing to work together and take on additional responsibility beyond their normal jobs
8. Effective written and verbal communication inside and outside the business
9. Consensus with external stakeholders to embrace your plan...you must have buy in
10. Following your plan...even in the face of adversity or opposition

KPI's and Metrics

Metrics are also known as "Key Performance Indicators" or (KPI's). KPI's are a formal business indicator that measures the Plan's performance to desired Goals. Behind each KPI listed below in parenthesis is a unique "metric" and the desired "direction".

1. $ Cash on hand ($ - increasing)
2. Net cash ($ - increasing)
3. Days cash certainty going forward (days - increasing)

4. Days of business life left (days - increasing)
5. Avg. days payable beyond terms (days - decreasing)
6. $ Payable beyond terms ($ - decreasing)
7. $ Unplanned cash needs ($ - decreasing)
8. Total Revenues ($ - increasing)

The above provides a sort of "Dash Board of KPI's" for Managers to know business performance to targets goals. I recommend that you initially keep it simple. From day one track what is important....#1 "$ Cash On Hand" and, #2, " Net Cash". These two measures will tell you a lot.

#1 is "how much blood supply (cash) do we have".

#2 is "what direction is the cash flow moving...up or down".

The others are in some cases variants of 1 and 2 and give different perspectives of the situation. Take special care to monitor and improve #3, "Days cash certainty going forward". This metric tells you how far into the future your cash horizon has absolute certainty. You plan future expenditures with this cash certainty horizon and therefore it must be realistic. To obtain that certainty, numbers must be accurate.

All good efforts worth doing should begin with a "Plan"

The old axiom says, "If you don't know where you are going, any road will get you there"...this timeless wisdom could never be more true then in the case of Crisis Cash Management. For this reason, I have included in Part 2 a Plan Template that you can use to prepare your own specific "Crisis Cash Flow Management Plan." You will find the Plan beginning at the bulkhead called Part 2 of this book. For now let's just accept it is there without diving into it. I want you to know "what and why", before "how". We also need to know when we have arrived so here are some thoughts to consider.

Has my business accomplished the mission?

You need to know when your business has accomplished the task of crisis cash management so let's set the "end goal" of a cash managed state.

Your business has accomplished effective cash flow management when:

1. **Skills, process and end state of "crisis cash management" are understood across the organization**
2. **Roles, responsibilities and accountability are defined to ensure success**
3. **Fundamental axioms of cash management and handling money effectively during a declining business or marketplace are understood and applied**
4. **The Crisis Cash Management Plan is in place and functioning**
5. **Critical success factors are understood and applied as KPI's**

6. **Crisis cash flow management is an ongoing core competency of the business**
7. **Recorded cash inflows and outflows produce a high degree of cash confidence**
8. **You plan for, (and have in place the infrastructure to support), maximizing inflow**
9. **All cash outflows are planned at a very granular level using a defined cash priority system**
10. **All payments for current and long term business obligations are timed with income**
11. **You use only cash you actually have on hand to pay for current and long term obligations...no added debt or limited added credit with extreme controls**
12. You can identify, monitor and control in advance, all cash flow risks such as loss of income, projected cash needs and fluctuations in the market
13. Peace of mind has occurred due to increased control over your cash situation (to the best degree possible under the given circumstances)
14. Drama and emotional changes stemming from a lack of cash control in the enterprise are low

If you answered "NO" to any of the above there is still work to be done. Items in bold must be accomplished by week one of your Plan execution. The balance will be ongoing results.

How can I get stakeholders "onboard" and add their support?

You have to agree, it's a bit "naive" to think that direct stakeholders are not already aware of your cash problems. They likely live with these problems and are effected by them daily...perhaps more than you ever will know. Involve stakeholders in all key decisions.

People support what they believe in.

If you want people to rally behind your cause, including saving your company, then treat them that way. Don't keep information from key stakeholders if you want them to "buy-in' with their support. Honesty, Honesty, Honesty. Massive research shows stakeholders will support most initiatives when they believe they are part of the solution and treated honestly and fairly.

Ownership of the initiative, (even partial ownership), allows employees to become involved logically...as well as emotionally in the outcome of the initiative, (the mission). Positive emotions drive stakeholders to excel for the good of your company. You can turn negative emotions into positive change. How do I accomplish this, you might be asking?

Get them involved from the start. Hold short and regular "stand up" meetings with each level of the enterprise. By "stand up" I mean get to the point by holding a meeting where everyone is standing, this will help get to the point. Meetings should be held daily at first with key direct stakeholders and then weekly once things begin to improve. Above all, "COMMUNICATE" with your staff, bank and employees. Use your KPI's and their running change as the topics of the meetings. Distribute charts showing progress and why negative issues are surfacing. At least explain the following and adjust as topics as conditions change:

1. Where are we now
2. How does this initiative effect me and my position
3. Where are we going and how will we get there
4. When will we get there and how will we know when we are there
5. What is going to change and how is that change going to affect me
6. What under my control are you asking me to do specifically
7. What is in it for me if I follow your leadership since I have alternative choices

Establish a sense of urgency, communication and honesty with personnel.

Incentives

Now some of you might be saying "I pay them a good wage or salary, why do I need to offer an incentive for my people to do their work". The answer is you don't.... but it helps.

Understand that you are motivating people to do more, do it better and make YOUR priorities THEIR priority. This goes beyond the present job description, employee relations, what you owe them or what they owe you. This is about saving your business.

"Incentives" always bring out the best performance from people. Be creative and offer something that **equals** the contribution you are asking from them or the effort they are being asked to make. Incentives are a wonderful way of letting people know you care.

People, (employees, suppliers, investors, management), act out of what is in their best personal interest. They don't mind "taking one for the team", (meaning giving up something temporarily), providing they see a means to be rewarded for doing so. This is the time to be highly creative. The list of possible incentives you could produce are endless. To start your thinking, I have compiled a short list to cover some more creative thoughts.

1. Give time off.
2. Cash...Money talks and I know cash is a critical resource right now, but formalize a plan to pay back what they may give initially as a free effort.
3. Bringing in lunch to reward small wins...like the day you reverse a declining cash position or when the Plan is fully operational and the reports are coming in.
4. Throw a modest function or event to reward large positive changes in your cash position.
5. Give away products or services when people can use them and recognize the value of the gift...not everyone can use a new widget or service, but sometimes companies are in a business where this is possible.

6. Add value in some way to their daily work at the firm like buy a new copier to replace the one that is a constant source of trouble. Have something they use every day redecorated, install a lunch area...you get the point.
7. Find something special that says we honor your contribution such as a beautiful pen, shirts, duffel bags, desk items, key chains...you know promotional items that have a real value...not some trinket that goes in the trash when your not looking.

I should share with you a personal experience of how "good" incentives work and a "teachable moment" in timing those incentives.

> I was VP of Supply Chain for a major multi-national shipbuilding firm with some 22 shipyards. I was asked by the CEO to join a KPMG "company wide initiative as a member of the core team". That effort would dramatically change the way business was being handled and improve efficiency in large ways. Out of a company of some 20,000 employees, only some ten people were involved in the Core Team...each coming from different business units, functions and management. My discipline happened to be supply chain and for several reasons including ongoing efforts, I just could not hand off an assignment of this magnitude to any else. I knew it was going to add at least 3-4 hours a day to my already high workload. I was already overseeing a major ERP-IT initiative at the time and was consolidating business units and purchasing functions weekly.
>
> As a Top Executive, I received stock options and bonuses and the normal compensations of a Senior Manager of a large company....after all, I was managing directly or indirectly the entire spend of the company's cash resources. I was fully behind the initiative and would have done it "gratis" just to see the increase in efficiency occur. What I did not know going in, was an incentive tied to the effort that I could take to the bank in the form of a check. After months and months of work and some significant gains, the core team was invited to a nice dinner at a fancy water front restaurant. At that dinner the CEO gave each one of us the equivalent of three months gross pay in a check...taxes paid. (Yes IRS, the revenue and taxes were shown in my returns that year!). I did not expect it...nor was I looking for it. I just wanted the company to succeed and my position along with it.

From this story, there are two key points about this compensation event.

1. One, is that incentives work best when people know about them before the actual effort is made.,
2. Second, unexpected gifts are a delight. (Just ask your wife or husband!)

I recommend you mix up #1 and #2 when possible. One being giving something of value unexpectedly. Second and not too far in the future, a large and recognizable "carrot" for accomplishing what is needed when the work is achieved.

OK. I was mistaken. The above can be added to.

1 Incentives that never happen, or, are just too far off in the future to be realized in the short term, are of little, or no perceived value.

We all need short wins. Set an incentive that is achievable. Remember that first kiss and the way it made you feel later on as you considered the future. Incentives...

2 The worse mistake in the world for a manager is to promise something of value and then find excuses why that incentive cannot be delivered. Credibility with management and life is essential. It is how I manage people and I can say with some pride that most all of the hundreds of employees that have been under my control gave their best...good times and bad.

Suppliers

Suppliers are critical external stakeholders to your recovery. Is it any wonder that Suppliers are critical to the success of your Crisis Cash Flow Plan? I hope not, as they can, and will, shut you down if they think that is the best way to getting a portion of their money. I am writing a huge book on sales which I will tell you about at the end of this portion of the Guide, but for now let's say that **suppliers can make, or break, a recovery effort.**

Further on, you will come across a section called **Paying Late** which goes into greater specifics on Suppliers and their willingness to help you increase your cash flow.

My goal for this section on suppliers is to make you aware of some key aspects where a supplier can assist you during the recovery effort. Suppliers want their money as they have bills to pay too, but are usually more than willing to listen if the message has high mutual benefit. This point is important and worth restating. **Your message has to be a balanced one in which you highlight the benefit for the supplier and the benefit for your firm if they help.**

Let's look at 15 key roles and possibilities for suppliers related to your recovery and your plan:

1. They are stakeholders of your success...albeit external
2. They have the legal right to close your business for non-payment if they can prove insolvency...(not paying your bills is insolvency)
3. Suppliers can increase your inventory in ways that will surprise you (e.g. vendor owned and/or vendor managed inventory)
4. They can delay payments
5. They can absorb debt for the good of the relationship
6. They can shift ownership of the product on the fly thus reducing your debt
7. They can stop inbound material with a phone call
8. They can open doors for new customers
9. They bring new and better technology to the table
10. They are a key source of market information
11. They can help solve internal problems
12. They can and should be a partner and collaborator in any recovery plan you develop
13. Suppliers can contribute both product and labor

14. They can legally take back product sitting on your shelf if they are not paid on time
15. They bring best practices to the table and can offer assistance in ways not thought of internally

Emotional times require a "level head"

Crisis conditions are an emotionally charged time. Try to handle emotional issues with ***calm resolve.*** As manager or owner, you have the authority to get control of the enterprise and the means to make positive changes resulting in an informed decision to stay in business profitably, sell it, or shut it down with the least impact on stakeholders.

You might be asking, "Jim, why are you using a "People Perspective"? Because people inside and outside the organization are concerned about the future and rightly so. The business is not running right and about this time in the cash decline cycle, turmoil and fear is setting in. That fear could be about their losing their jobs, housing, lifestyle and much more "off your management radar screen".

It is not wise to invalidate peoples comments and feelings with short comments that show a lack of basic concern. Work through your employees concerns if possible, or take them "off line" to a time when they can be dealt with in the quiet of your office...or even off site. It is essential you validate their feelings and become, (if your not already), a beacon of light in their stability...even if the world is falling apart around you. They will look to you for leadership and stability anyway, so be that person and demonstrate command and control over the crisis. Be methodical, talk in a low controlled voice and stay visible and in the forefront...not locked away in your office holding private meetings.

> *In my belief, God is not worried about how or if things will work out...He is much bigger than the problems facing you. Turn your troubles over to God, ask for His guidance in all decisions and ask for His blessings. Keep Him first in place your life. I know without a shadow of doubt that there is peace through Christ and abundant blessings for those who seek Him. No matter what is happening in the natural world.*

Stakeholders will do most anything to save their income if you ask nicely and show you have command over the situation. Reward them well when they do save your "hind end".

Decreasing spend velocity

The size of the company, its business maturity level and present spend activity largely control how fast the velocity of spend is moving out of the company...and therefore, in reverse...influence how long it will take to slow the velocity down. All businesses have a form of spending velocity which always seems to rise when times are good. **You must understand on "day-one" of your recovery that velocity of**

spend must be cut back once the decision to control and manage cash flow is made.

"Applying the brakes on spend" might be easy for a small company with one or two key spenders. You just talk it out and stop spending. However, in a large multi-level, multi divisional company, it might take several days to get the word across the entire firm down to people who really influence the cash outflow equation. Believe me, I know from personal experience how hard just getting to word out can be....let alone having complete conformance to the last dollar.

I should focus your thinking a bit. Moving spend from one allocation to another is NOT Stopping Spending...it is simply "reallocation" of the same limited resources to another place. "Stopping the Bleeding" means that on day-one you **STOP SPENDING ALL CASH.** Not just the larger cash outflows, but the smaller ones too. This will give the business an immediate cash boost as liabilities stack up over a couple of days. I do not mean stopping Payroll deposits or payroll taxes.

Surely, a business needs to spend money to stay alive and grow. **But, all spending from this point forward needs to be on a strictly "must have or else" basis.** This is a critical issue in crisis cash management. "Should have" spending should be allocated to only those expenditures which are tied directly to immediate cash inflow.

If the expense does not produce excess cash in the form of profits in the immediate near term, then why do it.

Looking longer out on the time horizon, normally there no cash available for long term investments during cash crisis condition. "Like to have" spending must be eliminated completely in the initial stages and then controlled "with an iron fist" in the longer term

Nothing should be done to increase cash outflow until the cause, or causes of cash flow decline are controlled, rectified and abated.

If you fail at stopping the cash outflow and reverse the negative cash flow margin, you will watch your company fail.

CCM is like a long tunnel with few paths that lead to recovery and many, many opportunities to see it all come hopelessly undone.

Setting spend priorities

There are many methods available to set priorities of spend. I introduced one methodology under the "must buy", "should buy" and "like to buy" ranking method I tend to use. This three tier method is very effective at placing spend controls into the Plan....but there are others.

The downside is that "must buy" is a very large bucket. It is quite possible you will need to break down the "must buy"" group into much smaller bites of spend in order to set spend priorities. To do so will require an even finer method of resource allocation priority. Therefore, to achieve a finer look at the world of spend, I recommend the following priority order as a means to break down "must have" spending:

1. Top Priority is Payroll (e.g. labor, including your own). This a debt you have already incurred and peoples lives depend on the payment. If you need to reduce payroll then act, and act fast. I will cover this more later under "Reduction in Force".
2. Next is obviously payroll taxes as the payroll tax man can and will shut you down faster than you can say "Pork" for not paying in.
3. Next is payments for spend that produce immediate cash in hand...(I do not mean termed payment sales, I mean you exchange the product or service and receive cash or a very good check that becomes cash today.)
4. Next is spend that supports the production of "immediate cash". I buy this today and sell it today or tomorrow thinking. Spend that will produce cash in the current (week, month).
5. Next is Spend that when combined with existing resources, (say labor, a service or asset item), produce immediate cash.
6. Next is incurred debt repayment. This item could be Point #1 or #2 on our list depending on the ability to re-negotiate terms and link it to Point #3. These are your typical suppliers.
7. Next is spend that will produce cash BEFORE the bill is actually due for the spend needed to make it, do it, or deliver it.
8. Next is longer range spend like property taxes, some pre-negotiated debt etc....normally places where automatic terms apply if you don't pay on time. (Keep in mind this is short term credit folks, not "manna from heaven" because you can push it off till later. Later does come.)
9. Spend that produces cash with longer payment terms. Lacking any other option, I would rather receive payment later, than no payment at all.

The above "must buy" priority list can be adjusted to suit with the end goal of protecting what little cash you have on hand and increasing cash production.

When cash is low or absent, the "should buys and "like to buys" will have to wait.

One Final Experienced Observation: I think it is wrong to hold off one supplier while you pay for the same product through another supplier. It is underhanded... yet legal...for a while. I think it is much better to work out a solution with the existing supplier to keep the inflow of products and services coming. It builds trust and stronger supplier relationships. Don't go behind their back for the same product you normally bought from them....they always find out and relationships are taxed if not abandoned.

Cash Inflow (Receipts)

"Cash Inflow" is all monies received by the company in the normal course of business and through crisis recovery actions. This includes routine payments for goods and services, loan receipts, interest received on balances, sale of assets, etc.

Some cash is received at the point of sale, some is received on a time basis such as monthly. Some is directly tied to the completion of a transaction or phase of work completed, as in projects. What we need to recognize is that the time of payment figures heavily into the entire cash flow picture.

With cash inflow, we need to understand and monitor all "anticipated or planned" cash that is inbound to the company regardless of source in order to obtain cash flow accuracy. We do this by creating a "cash inflow schedule" that represents two key figures..."planned" and "actual" cash on hand.

Actual is what cash is in hand or cleared by the bank. Planned is what income is "booked", but not yet turned into actual "go to the bank and withdraw it" cash. The important distinction between the two is that planned cash inflow is not yet "real money". It is a promise to pay, (or) a payment made but not yet cleared.

You can only spend cash money actually in your possession...no matter who is running the books

Imagine you've deposited a business check and wrote out a business check thinking the check would clear in time. With a credit line or cash cushion in the bank account sufficient to cover the check you write...it's not a problem. However, in a "cash crisis", our cash cushion (the reserves) is becoming low or is even gone entirely. If anything disrupts the check deposit processing, or you need to cover an emergency with other cash, your check would certainly not clear. The entity who received your NSF bad check would not have the confidence in your ability to pay your debts nor would they likely want another check to cover the first, as that second check is just another "promise to pay".

The usual request once a check doesn't clear is a friendly "cash or bank check for your company check". Further, it is against the law in the U.S. to write bad checks on any purchase or debt payment. This is important:

A bad check is legal evidence your business is technically insolvent and that proof will stand up in a court of law as hard evidence.

You want to be able to tell anyone, (even though your business is suffering significant cash problems), that your checks are good and tied to actual cash...not booked to some "maybe we will get some cash in time for your check".

You would be surprised how far suppliers will extend credit when they know with 100% certainty that what they sell to you will be paid for...no matter what...and without adding any personal guarantees. A lot depends on how you act with the supplier.

Let's get back to the cash inflow schedule as inflow is our new "blood supply" of cash. We want the longest financial view we can obtain. The numbers we post must be accurate, factual and very, very, realistic. No room for "blue sky" or overconfidence here. Revenue should only be entered as "Booked Revenue" when it is actually sold. Otherwise it is a "Planned Revenue". I am not discounting Planned Revenue as it's good to know the long term cash horizon, but you need a provision to know the difference between Booked revenue and Planned revenue. In a spreadsheet all this is easy as you can record the entries as they are and as they change status. I use separate columns which allows me to total each condition as the status changes.

Corrections and changes to the information must be recorded immediately when found or as an entries change. The most important condition for this is when an entry changes from booked revenue to actual cash in the bank. Your spreadsheet should always be exactly accurate...otherwise you are "flying blind". Again, the cash inflow schedule should be the closest you can get to actual REALITY. It might seem like a lot of work to keep this up and most companies run some form of this as they record sales and reconcile bank deposits.

Below, I will talk about making improvements in the schedule content values. For now, let's say you have an idea of what the cash inflow schedule looks like and how important it is to keep current and accurate. Let's move on to some thoughts that improve cash inflow. After all we need "new blood" and lots of it.

Collecting Early

All new sales and all "in process" sales with terms of payment should be advanced forward in time of cash receipt collection whenever possible so as to increase cash margins. Advancing inflow makes no change in the inflow quantity, but by collecting early, the cash flow margin increases over what it would have been if it was not advanced. In contrast delays work the opposite way.

Offering **prompt pay discounts** is a great way to move receivables forward in time of payment. If your customers are paying later than 10 days, they should be targeted to advance their payables. Try meeting with your key 30+day term payment customer and offer him or her a 2% Net 10 discount. This is a great motivational tactic for large and small companies. For large company customers 1% discount will not do it...neither will 1.5%. But 2%...yes! For your company, a receivable that is collected in 10 days is a much faster cash turnover. If you were on a 45-60 day payment schedule, the change in net cash flow from prompt pay initiatives would be the sum of all receipts advanced.

Gross Average Method: Take the sum of what you have sold the customer over 12 months, divide that figure by 365. This result equals net average receipts/day. Take that result and multiply that figure by the number of days you moved the receipts forward. This is the added cash flow you can get from advancing the term of payment forward.

Now imagine this system across your entire payables. In a couple of days you could change your entire outlook on accelerating cash flow.

Note: If you sell to the Government, they have to fill in a lot of paper work if they do not take a prompt pay discount. In simple terms, the Government would rather pay in 10 days, than fill out the mountain of paperwork justifying why they did not take the prompt pay discount. I have sold many times to the Government and I was always paid in 15 days tops. It works...most every time.

Late paying customers:

Now is a good time to talk about customers who routinely pay late...beyond your agreed terms.

In my humble opinion, these customers should pay a premium for that right of extended credit. Offer them a cash discount incentive designed to move their payments forward or, consider raising your price to compensate for the extended credit. If a customer wants to lean on your credit, you might as well receive higher compensation for the delay in payment than they could get at a bank for financing their payments and being on time. I tell customers in a nice way of course, why they are getting a separate line item on their bill for financing late payment beyond agreed terms. Most times your receipts will suddenly not be late.

Charging More

Charging more, (receiving more revenue, "getting more new blood"), involves several approaches.

The first approach is to increase prices. I suggest all price increases take place in very small increments, unless you are just far below market prices. Small increases are almost not even noticed by the average customer except on very sensitive commodity based items.

Raising prices is hard to do during down times. Try to get even a little more revenue for what you do, (if it is at all possible). Yes, I know raising prices may not be always an option, but if you can raise prices just the equivalent of $2.74/day, spread across all your sales for the day, the result would be an extra $1,000 over an annual term. What could a small business do right now with an extra $1,000? In a small business, that increase could finance a small capital equipment purchase, or be the difference of keeping a good employee working. Need more...how about $10,000 or $100,000 more income per year? Well that works out to be $27.40/calender day and $274.00/calender day respectfully. Remember, your increase is spread across all sales, not just a single transaction. These figures do not sound like much of an increase per day to me...but I am not steering the ship. You are.

The second approach is to expand your service offerings anyway possible, providing you are being paid for it of course. I think the biggest issue with service offerings is that revenue is linked to the time spent delivering the service. For those of you traveling to deliver a service, try to sell some "value added services" that allow you to remain on the customer site longer and be paid for it. In on site services, the biggest issue is the unpaid downside of set up and tear down time. It makes no money, so the longer you are on site delivering services, the more income you can receive.

In opposite to providing more service, is a cost reduction activity called "customer self service". This is offering a service the customer does for themselves. You enable the service, say online, or at a Kiosk, but the service is actually performed by the customer.

Lowering Costs of Goods Sold (COGS):

The reversal of *Charging More* is reducing costs to produce a good or deliver a service. Below are some cost reduction opportunities for the seller because of a predictable buyer or demand:

- Money is spent on improving the relationship, not obtaining a new one.
- Demand Forecasts allow sellers to better meet fixed and variable schedules.
- Greater efficiency in individual transactions.
- A predictable long range "base of business" allow sellers to plan resources, allocate assets and plan expansion programs.
- Waste is designed out of the overhead, sales, and value delivery process saving money for both sides....it is called "Lean"
- Transactional cost reduction.
- Manufacturing cost reduction.
- Service delivery cost reduction.
- Indirect expense reduction.

In the upcoming section on "Paying Less" I am going to show you how one dollars in savings is worth one hundred dollars in sales.

In a cash crisis this important area cannot be overlooked. However, it is normally an involved process. There are "low hanging fruit" in this area and this is the only target I would be looking at during the initial recovery.

Book: "The 10 Reasons Why Buyers Don't Buy"

In my latest book titled **"The 10 Reasons Why Buyers Don't Buy"** (© Jim Rohr 2009) soon will be available at www.amazon.com and other fine book retailers, I cover extensive cost reduction strategies, cost issues and business value improvement in this huge Book. This incredible knowledge resource took over three years to write and is packed with hundreds of suggestions on ways to overcome The 10 Reasons Why Buyers Don't Buy. Check back with your retail book sales outlet or order an advance copy today at leading bookstores.

Cash Outflow (Disbursements)

Negative cash flow is the ultimate death of a business enterprise. The enterprise lives on cash flow, just like the human body lives on blood (cash) and blood pressure (cash flow). Cash outflow must be controlled if the enterprise is to survive.

Cash Outflow Reduction, (if not a complete halt of cash outflow), is essential is essential to launch the initial recovery of the business enterprise. Without slowing, reducing, or stopping cash outflow to gain control of the company, all new cash infusions whether from "capital loans", or "asset sales", or "supplier credit" will do nothing but postpone the eventual death of the enterprise as the underlying causes have not been arrested or lessened in impact and event.

The financial difference between "cash inflow actual" and "cash outflow actual" is your present Net Cash Position measured in dollars, yen or other currency. Therefore, collecting more cash earlier, or paying cash out later, (and hopefully in less amounts), will improve your cash flow margin. Let's look at the role of each one.

Paying Late

If early collection of outstanding revenues, (getting cash in early), advances one side of the cash flow equation, then paying late (cash outflow), certainly boosts the other side of the same equation.... Before you jump off paying everybody later than agreed, understand that paying late is a double-edged sword.

On one side, even a small increase in payment terms will make a big difference in cash flow. On the other hand, this increases the outstanding debts of the firm and places an "unplanned" burden on your supplier.

Unless spend is very controlled, spend will usually, (...but not always), rise to the level of credit the company has or obtains.

With qualified companies, Suppliers are usually willing to extend credit terms to obtain sales. When the terms extend beyond their credit policy, suppliers demand payment or expect greater control on your enterprise for the extension of time.

Notes payable for a leveraged firm is usually a good place to start looking for delays in payments. They generally are one of the largest periodic outflows of cash and the relationships are usually better. Terms are usually bank controlled based on your credit capacity. When times get tough, Banks would rather extend additional terms, (for a fee of course), instead of losing the asset income. In all cases, see what creditors are willing to do...even temporarily, such as a delay in payment.

A delay, (postponement of a payment for a month or so), has the net effect of increasing cash flow during the delayed month. Work with your suppliers, and if possible, get them to accept a firm delayed payment. This can be accomplished any number of ways, but if you have difficulty paying a bill, call your key suppliers and ask them for a delay in payment. Tell them you are getting control of your cash disbursements, putting in a new system and will be able to tell them the exact day payment can be made with 100% confidence. Tell them you want to make absolutely sure you issue a check with cash certainty. Most will understand and agree on the spot, but don't be one second late with your payment if they agree. Paying on time after some delay adds confidence that they can rely on your business and you are not a "dead beat".

Let's back up a second and look at what is going through the minds of suppliers. Suppliers are in a precarious position. They extended credit to a company on the promise to pay under agreed terms....normally their internal policy and your creditworthiness. As your business declines and your payments extend, this agreed position for the supplier weakens. All they want is their money and you to succeed... read that as "buy more products and services". But suppliers have bills to pay too and a business to run so there are limits...stated and unstated.

Here is my list of supplier options available in the normal course of business in collection of unpaid debt. These are ranked by escalating priority starting with the highest desirable normal relationship and moving down in relationship and options:

1. Vendor installed inventory
2. Vendor owned inventory
3. Vendor managed inventory
4. Growing business with your company at agreed terms
5. Sustaining existing business with your company at agreed terms
6. Managing declining business with your company at agreed terms
7. Extending terms of payment to keep current business (at a cost to someone)
8. Extending terms to get paid on a promise date
9. Paying for past product on the promise of new product
10. Moving the account to COD (Cash on Delivery)
11. Moving the account to CIA (Cash in Advance)
12. Taking back product to help offset outstanding debt
13. Accepting a reduced amount for quick cash collection
14. Taking back the used or unused product and calling the account as closed
15. Accepting an unrelated asset for the amount due
16. Moving the account to collections
17. Moving the account to legal action to recover a debt
18. Force bankruptcy

I have seen a supplier sue a company over a debt, win in court after some heated battle, then in the hall of the court after the judgment was announced, ask the buyer for new business opportunities. You just never know what will be the outcome. So be open to creative opportunities to settle and move forward at any time in the process. Both parties want the relationship to succeed but the power moves to the supplier once the item is sold to your company.

Suppliers, employees and creditors each have the legal right to foreclose on a enterprise that is not paying their bills on time.

Paying Less

Sometimes you can cut costs in the near and long term by paying less for what the business buys. It has a dramatic effect to your bottom line...dollar for dollar. Let me restate this for those not familiar with supply chain lingo and purchasing savings.

Nothing...not increased sales...increased cash collection or bringing on new products has the impact dollar-for-dollar that cost reduction has.

Here is the example I referred to in an earlier section. Suppose your after tax profit margin is about 4%. Now pay attention. To earn $4 of net income you need to sell $100 worth of something.

Now, with cost reductions, it is a entirely different story. Let's say you save $4 through some means. If you save $4, you don't need to sell, make, deliver and get paid late that $100. WOW.

Every dollar saved in COGS goes directly to the bottom line of the company.

Paying less, is a reduction in the cost of materials, sales, administration, and/or labor consumed or used by the enterprise. Careful shopping for best price is but one answer.

One affective way to reduce cost, is aggregation of spend through a single supplier. If your purchases are scattered between two, three or more suppliers for a single item, consider aggregating the entire spend to one supplier for a deep discount. Make sure you select the right supplier, as this is not something done without a high confidence in the selected supplier, forethought and contracts.

"Strategic Sourcing" and "Target Costing" are best practices designed to reduce costs of materials and services that the enterprise uses by leveraging the spend of the firm. These methods employ intense efforts in every section of the business to "lean out" hidden costs and process costs.

Say you're a small company and your total spend is divided across a number of suppliers. Combined, your spend doesn't amount to much of anything...let alone through one product or service category. What can you do to reduce costs? I will give you some hope.

First, in an economic crisis, consider that your suppliers sales are also down. They also have a company to run and a company to help survive."Three bids and a buy" is still good basic advise until more strategic purchasing programs can come online. Look for win-win strategies together such as ways to reduce transactional costs, apply vendor managed inventory, increase forecasting, etc. Suppliers will be interested in anything that cuts down on their internal costs and improves their relationship with customers.

Try meeting with suppliers face to face with frank discussions like, "We are trying to survive and prosper and we need your help." You will often find a willingness to work out almost anything...including extending terms, lowering their prices and foregoing some debt, all in order to keep even reduced revenue flowing to them. Flowing revenue is a side of cash flow management for them too.

Now I know I skipped lightly through this section and to do it justice would take more, far more. But for now, I want you to open up to the supplier on real issues and ask for help. The rest can come when time and resources allow.

Temporary or Permanent Pay Cuts

Temporary or permanent cuts in pay ("Pay Reduction") is a short-term solution to reduce the cost of the same labor received; however, this tactic should be used quite sparingly. Actually, I prefer to view reductions in pay as reduced labor cost on book in the short term and long term as a future obligation of the company to be paid back when funds allow. I recommend working out a different strategy than "across-the-board" pay cuts.

Over the years I have shifted my thinking to balancing cost of labor through team consensus. When possible, (and it is not always possible), I have the employee management team come up with the necessary changes to improve cash flow and profitability through many methods...including reducing the cost of labor or balancing the cost of labor to the income streams available. These efforts are done in conjunction with a direct edict type goal I create that achieves the end goal required for financial stability. If I need to reduce labor cost by 20%, I say so...then the team takes over.

Communicate the goals to the team upfront. You would be surprised at the creative nature of some labor teams. I have seen them reduce salaries, go to a four day work week, anything that sustains the available personnel energy capital. Sometimes the team identifies how to best handle the situation and meet target goals through careful inspection of each employee's ability to contribute. People have other issues outside the company and some would love to have say a Monday off to handle them. Others need a few hours on Tuesday and Friday to take their child, mother or husband somewhere important. Others would like to attend class in school on certain days. You would be surprised at the creativity when people are given the chance to control their contributions and reduce the overall impact.

Bear in mind that this approach of "self direction" does not always work and it needs direct hands on oversight by senior management during the decision making process, but as long as you are open to suggestions and are creative...right here is a great place to learn about the company from their eyes and begin working together for a common solution. It is far better for the team to come up with a strategy for pay and labor reduction with immediate "buy-in", instead of you cramming something down everyone's throat under the fear of losing your job.

Set a time limit of say 2 days for them to come up with the strategy. Give them clear goals and let them work it out. Give them all the time they need, but you need to give them a fall back solution. If their plan does not achieve the end goal and meet the companies needs, your fall back plan will kick in automatically. Employees need to know you are going to have control no matter what, but they also need to know they are given free reign to come up with a workable solution.

In labor relations, pay reduction is never "free"

You might consider **reducing pay, (without a change in labor force), as being the same as an employee extending some future credit to the company.** Asking someone to do the same, (no, do more because of the need for higher output), than they did yesterday, (and for less pay), is leveraging the employee/employer relationship unfairly in my humble opinion. I think at best this is a one sided exchange.

Pay reduction is a form of contribution that advances the company's interests...albeit at the expense of the employee. This time the contribution is not coming from a bank, it is coming from your employee. To balance the field I record the reductions as long term debt so when "times of plenty" return, I would pay them back for that contribution in time, money, or both. If the company moves towards closure, I can always move the employee debt back into current obligations through a Journal Entry. This gives them a much better position in bankruptcy proceedings. Decisions are captured in the Corporate Minutes so it cannot be challenged by other creditors during bankruptcy as an invalid debt. Let's drop back for a second and look at this issue a bit deeper.

Every position within your company from the floor sweep to the CEO is a pre-negotiated exchange of work for compensation. For non-senior managers, this is pay check without employment incentives and golden parachutes. At the end of the day all they have to show for their hard work is a paycheck.

It's true, employees will contribute to the success of the enterprise by taking a pay reduction, but will only do so for a short time…say up to one half year, or perhaps a bit longer if the positive end is in sight and not part of a wide spread economic downturn. Once pay reductions begin, most aggressive and better employees will move on to better jobs elsewhere unless they see a noticeable improvement in the conditions quickly. Their options are not as limited as middle employees or pure labor employees.

I would make every effort to pay back the employees when good times returned.

I have found if you compensate an employee fairly in the give and take scenario, you will bond them emotionally to the company...sometimes for life. Besides, it is treating our fellow man fairly...and that is what I feel Jesus would do.

Reduction in Force (RIF)

Another method to reduce costs is dreaded layoffs or **Reduction in Force (RIF).** It seems like companies everywhere are cutting labor. My personal experience in this is far more then I care to admit.

I once cut 40% of the work force of a large plant on a single day and came out the other end producing 40% more product. I know how hard it is to make this decision, but that is what managers must do...make hard decisions that effect peoples lives.

Here we need to clarify the difference between losing unproductive people and having a general layoff because of company downturn, regardless of reason. These two goals can be mutually inclusive. I assume you are making RIF decisions based on the difference between "unproductive employees" and "employees worth saving" and balancing the labor pool to production needs. In a cash crisis, the RIF event is tied to a reduced need for labor. In a "leaning" initiative with the same output, a Reduction in Force requires that the same labor work smarter, (and harder), to produce the same output, (products and services), that it once did with more employees.

If your company is labor intensive, anything you can do to reduce labor costs will translate to large bottom line savings, dollar for dollar. This is the upside of having less payroll. Unfortunately RIF also has a down side.

Reductions in Force are quite hard on the person leaving the company for sure. A RIF is also damaging to those left behind who have mixed feelings of being saved... and perhaps being the next target. In larger companies, several RIF initiatives may take place as they bring the labor pool down. Some companies move up and down in labor like a yo-yo. In less volatile companies, the cost of replacing quality people is fairly high...some HR types estimate this as high as 90% of annual salary. I tend to agree when the position is complex. There is always a real cost for bringing on a new employee.

It might be possible to use excess "RIF Target people" in such a way as to increase sales, reduce costs, or other "out of the box" thinking. It is very disarming to customers to be called upon by non-sales employees. Sometimes their "non-sales speak" can open doors your best salesmen can't even budge. People speak at all levels and sometimes this is a great initiative. Now, I am not saying to put them in complex sales situation which have high risk, but you might use them to handle what they know. It's worth a try.

One last question that continues to perplex me over and over is, "Whatever happened to the implied moral obligation of company to employee and employee to company?" Is the current paradigm of "expendable people" really a lasting management practice or is something else resurfacing. I do know that winning companies are practicing employee dedication once again and it is very refreshing to see young and progressive CEO's rewriting the book on employee relations. Winning companies have employees dedicated to their success and the company is dedicated to their success as well from school, to child care, to free lunches, to gyms, to rest areas....it's thankfully a new day in Labor relations. Use RIF sparingly and only after all other options have been leveraged.

Reduction in overhead (non-personnel)

Reduction in overhead is essential to re-gaining financial health. All non-essential expenditures must be reduced and if possible...stopped. **These can include non-essential rentals, sub-contracting, utilities, insurance, benefits, perks, etc. This should be one area where your company should be the "leanest" possible.** I can almost always find reductions in expense by checking into this area and reducing overhead.

Get out your **schedule (accounting document) of overhead expenditures** and start looking behind the numbers. Ask lots of questions...starting with, "Why do we need this?" Then ask the same question five more times..."Is there something we can do to eliminate this expense?" After the fifth time, if you still need it, keep it. Otherwise, dump these expenses immediately.

Recall that I showed an earlier example where each dollar saved in COGS goes straight to the bottom line. Compare that to the work required to earn one dollar of "profit". A typical company has to sell $100 for every $4 it puts to the bottom line... after taxes. To earn $4,000, a company would need to sell $100,000 in services and product. There is a lot of effort and risk involved in selling $100,000 of anything to anyone.

On the flip side, a simple cost reduction of $4,000 per year means the company **would not** need to sell/make/earn that $100,000 in gross revenue. Perhaps you cannot find that $4,000, but with some initiative "releasing corporate wealth through reduction of cost," a company can boost the bottom line, dollar for dollar, with ever dollar saved. Is it making sense where the real money is besides selling more? I hope so.

Time is not on your side in a crisis.

Reduce COGS and work on increasing sales at the same time.

Moving the company

If you do decide to move your facility to "cheaper digs", (new location that costs less), be prepared to spend big bucks for all kinds of related "moving expenses".... some known and some well hidden from view. Make a very detailed assessment of all expenses involved in a move before pushing the "big green we need to move button". Lost momentum, lower revenue, confused customers, new deposits, build out costs and a bunch of other hidden expenses are some of the more likely drains on that limited cash you HAD in the bank. Here is an "experienced golden nugget".

A physical move usually finishes off a company in financial trouble because the decision to make the move happens far to late...when the company is at its' weakest financially.

Better to avoid this decision entirely, unless part of a formal turn around and new fresh resources are allocated to assist in the move and the recovery of market share. Make sure mega cash is available to pay for the move and adequate time is available to recover the lost sales momentum. Yes, I have moved a fair sized company over a single weekend and survived - so it can be done, but the effort and cash needed was incredible.

How should I handle emergency "unforeseen' expenditures

I provide in Part 2 a simple form your people can use to track unforeseen needs, (expenditures), and run an approval process. The form, (or some other solution), improves decision making and timing about these kind of expenditures. The form moves the expenditure onto the **cash outflow schedule.**

Basically, the **reactive** portion of our Crisis Cash Management Plan consists of capturing unanticipated or immediate cash needs that were not projected or fixed at the project level, or part of a business units' normal cash need projections. The form named "Cash Priority Request" or ("CPR"...pun intended!), was developed to aid in managing this cash disbursement process. If the cash need exists on the "projected" cash sheet normally rolled up from the project, business unit, division or corporate schedule, the form is not used. When it is used, and no other recording of the expense has been budgeted or allocated, the projected or fixed cash outflow schedule must be changed.

I repeat..."Nothing should be purchased outside the Crisis Cash Management Plan".

The CPR form is used for those expenses you did not know about or plan for.

One footnote to this issue. The form, by its very nature, acknowledges the cash described as a HIGH PRIORITY request, a "must have" expenditure. Time for decision and recommendations are all part of the data entered on the form. Forms may be sent electronically, or via fax, to the respective internal party for coordination and processing of when the cash will be available and records its approval. The form must follow a set procedure determined well in advance for handling and approval. In an automated IT world, the entire form and its processing can be fully automated....but who has money for that when the creditors are knocking on the door?

Putting in new cash (capital...financial blood) into the enterprise

Normally this means adding money...usually your personal money, or the banks money, or other peoples money...into the coffers of the business to meet its current and long term financial obligations.

Keep in mind that conservative outsiders, such as banks and investors, normally do not loan money to businesses in sharp decline. Those that do loan money to businesses in distress, make demands for that money. They lend only if the balance sheet shows they would have a very secure position if the business goes under. Collateral will normally be required to secure this type of loan. This is easier for an asset rich business whose assets can be sold quickly for the value of the loan...such as unburdened equipment and land.

The other condition is when an outsider takes an "investor position" in the firm. Here he would likely have his team manage a turn around, or the loan is directly tied to some other asset of high value....like your personal house. When people outside the organization take a management role you can bet the future is going to be full of sweeping changes... including your role in the firm. Let's go a bit deeper into "debt secured by collateral".

> **Side Bar**
>
> ***No personal money should ever go in to a company unless it is a secured loan to that company. Otherwise, it is a gift, an unsecured loan or a purchase of stock. Stock could become worthless and would be subordinate behind secured creditors. Be a secured creditor.***

Taking on collateral based debt

This is a huge topic and the variations of how, when and how much debt issued against collateral should be taken on are endless. Therefore, since I can't dive into the weeds on this one, I am going to issue some high level thoughts on crisis cash input based on collateral based debt. Of course, taking on more debt is ultimately a "gut call" as the balance of debt to income must make financial sense.

I am a very conservative business manager who is not afraid of taking calculated risks. I am NOT a firm believer in taking on more debt to save a dying business. This is one time to leave your "save the company at all cost" ego out of the equation. We are all human. Egos can and do cloud a normally good and sound financial decision. Before taking on more debt, I prefer to suspend the outflow of cash, assess the likelihood of recovery and then move forward...including investigating selling the business off.

Understand that debt, (all debt), comes with current and future obligations which are not what the struggling firm needs right now in recovery. Better to understand all the costs associated with recovery of the enterprise using a "very jaundice pen", understand the risks involved with saving the business, and then take on more debt only if there is 100% confidence in the ability of the money to positively and substantially impact the recovery outcome and the repayment of the debt. In the meantime you can leverage what credit you already have.

Leverage of bank and supplier credit

Usually this is the first place the enterprise reaches for a leveraged "cash lifeline". Bank lines of credit and Supplier Credit both become a source to bring needed cash into the enterprise.

The credit line is truly a key issue. Since it is already secured by some basis...normally your assets, personal, business or both. THINK HARD and then leverage it only to the degree needed to support a full recovery. The end results are the same three options.

Either you turn the business around and recover, or the business (and your personal assets) are lost to bankruptcy...or you sell out some or all of the business.

There are no other options.

Supplier credit is the terms of payment provided to a buying company by a supplier for the purpose of selling into your business. Thirty (30) days are the norm. Some suppliers will go longer if they feel secure in payment and desire your business. I have found that larger companies routinely pay forty five to sixty (45-60) days as a standard practice. Others never miss a supplier imposed deadline.

Most suppliers selling large volumes into the company will ignore small delays in payment. Other smaller suppliers are calling the company on day thirty one (31st) when the payment is not in hand. Still others will stop all future shipments until they have the payment in hand.

How far will a supplier extend credit and continue to sell into your company? That depends. Who knows what a supplier will agree with until you ask. I mentioned before and reemphisize here that suppliers are a vested stakeholder in your business and deserve to know what the future holds. I do know that suppliers are more willing to extend credit terms when they know up front what the future holds for them, than being a victim of a company taking extensions without their knowledge upfront. I feel companies who lean on supplier credit without a suppliers knowledge are not playing fair and will ultimately pay a price. This is not a decision which should be taken lightly.

Make sales which result in "real profit"

1. Why take the risk of accepting a questionably profitable order only to find out later that you lost money making, building or supplying the item. If you want to solve the problem of low cash, then make sure all sales and estimates reflect a high degree of "cost and profit certainty." Trading cash for cash, or "red ones for blue ones" as I say, makes absolutely no sense when on average

96% of that cash will ultimately move outside the company to down line suppliers and stakeholders.
2. Conserve your company's financial strength and sell profitably, with low risk, or not at all. You should know upfront (in advance of commitment to the order), if your firm is going to make money or lose money by accepting the sale.
3. Poor estimating of cost has been the ruin of many a business on the financial edge of survival.
4. Desperation leads to poor sales decisions and low or negative income.

Cost Control

Cost analysis and cost control best practices are beyond the scope of this Guide. Here, I am only highlighting a need to understand your true costs before accepting orders.

Budgets are essential to communicate to the shop floor what is necessary to make a profit. If you are going to track financial progress against your base line cost plan, you must compare the plan, (hopefully budget by task), to each production task. Everyone should know what the budget for the active job is...and how to work toward making and beating that budget.

If workers do not know the budget they are working to, (at the task level), how can they measure their performance.

Do some research into the advanced cost program of "Activity Based Costing", (ABC). This "best practice" allows you to understand all costs associated with producing a good or service in a way different than traditional cost accounting. This differs from GAAP approved recognition of costs, which does not recognize costs in a homogeneous manner. The effectiveness of the best practice is amazing and is a vehicle to reduce costs. Sure, in summary, even when applying ABC, on the GAAP Profit/Loss and Balance Sheet all costs do roll up. The hardest part of ABC is running two cost collection systems, but it is worth it.

ABC might not be something you want to jump into during the recovery stage, but it is something you should consider as part of a full turn around.

Selling off assets

Selling off assets is a big, big, decision...and normally an emotional decision too. Before you go off selling everything that matters, consider dividing your assets into three basic categories just like my proposed inventory classification:

- **Class A Assets:** Class A assets are all those things that make money...land, building, equipment, etc. These will be the last to sell and when these go, you can bet the company is going to be a lot smaller.
- **Class B Assets:** Class B assets are those things that are used occasionally, but do not fall into Class A status. It might not seem right, but anything used "oc-

casionally" is fair game to be sold off...normally at a fairly decent price. Now, if the item is essential to your processes, then selling it makes no sense unless you can reasonably rent the item...and you can rent a lot of stuff these days.

- **Class C Assets:** Class C assets include items like that old truck on the back lot that does not work for your business anymore...the steel "whatever" that is making rust and the tools that are tired or almost never get used. Basically, it includes working and non-working items that have no play in making money in the streamlined firm. It also includes miscellaneous scrap metal and items which can be sold for scrap metal. For me, it might include a collection of odd stuff I bought to one day restore to working condition. I am known to keep a lot of stuff because someday, I might need it...yes I am a pack rat. Now, if I could only find that scissor jack I bought at the yard sale.

In Part 2, we are going to review this category and there is a step to sell B and C off. For now start getting your A, B, C lists together.

Hint: Have someone take good quality photos of the items as they record the item for management. Number them as you go as an asset number. Photos save a lot of time and trouble visualizing the items for a second and third time. Plus you can use them when you offer them for sale.

Selling off inventory

Just like selling off assets, we are going to do the same A, B, C, classification system and sell off of unneeded inventory. The only difference here is that the inventory classification should be based on the number of turns the inventory makes per year. Inventory turns are the number of times the total inventory value for a specific item, (item # or SKU), are sold per year, month or other...normally a year.

I am going to use a typical inventory classification system that I have used in typical production companies. Therefore:

- Class A are items which turn faster than 8 times a year. (some companies would be thinking of 52 as a low number...like cell phone manufacturers)
- Class B are items which turn between 5 and 8 times a year.
- Class C are items which turn less than 5 times a year.

Here's my proposed plan:

1. Sort your inventory list into each Class Category. If you do not know what the turns are (and you should)...make an educated guess.
2. Now take the same list and make a customer list by each inventory class or item if necessary.
3. Starting at the bottom, we have Class C customers. Call these customers on the list and offer the entire list of items they use at a 50%-75% reduction... providing they will take all the entire list of items in one transaction. You need a fast answer.
4. Move on to Class B inventory items. These should sell between 50% and 75% of book value.

5. Lastly, Class A inventory is last to go. These will sell almost any day for between 75% and 90% of sale price (not book value).

Remember, we are trying to make cash and lots of it. Add the Class C asset revenue to your fall back cash account...everything else can go towards current obligations in order of cash outflow priority. Your "fall back account" is your last line of cash defense. It might be what you need to close the business down.

Expense Accounts and other traditional outflows

I am going to briefly discuss the subject of expense accounts and how they can be modified or tailored to suit conditions.

In simple language, all *travel is suspended and all expense privileges are suspended.*

"You're in a cash crisis", and unless the trip is going to sell 10% of your annual revenue or save the company...then don't take the trip and for goodness sake, don't spend anything through regular credit card channels that charge high interest.

You don't have the cash for lunches, dinners, books, training media, or anything else you used to charge on that card. If it does not make money today, than it is not needed...period. It's a cash crisis right?

Advertising

Oftentimes, companies have significant advertising programs running on television, radio, the Internet, magazines, billboards, and newspapers to name a few channels. While essential to sales, they can tax cash reserves and prohibit other more important responsibilities. Don't get the wrong idea. I believe in advertising...provided every advertising dollar spent delivers "traceable results". Why spend money in advertising if it doesn't produce traceable results?

Consider for a moment the logical flow of a general "consumer buying process". I follow the general process of **Awareness, Interest, Preference and Selection...**in that order. This was taught to me by my good friend, Bob Rehak, a marvel in business advertising and communication. Here I am going to talk only about the first two, Awareness and Interest. These are the main areas advertising can address best. If customers are not "aware" of your offerings, then they cannot decide if your offerings are of "interest" enough to prefer to select them. The interest part of the process comes from what you say and how.

If your customer base is made up of "walk ins," then you better continue some form of "in your face" advertising to let them know your alive, where you are and what you are offering. However, you might consider low cost alternatives to the formal billboards and radio. Some shops use a "low budget" A-Frame advertising board right at their store front road. The cost difference is incredible between the two channels. Consider a $300 one-time cost in place of the local $600.00/month billboard not counting the sunk costs of the billboard wrap itself. That $600 a month saved will go a long way towards financial survival...especially in a small firm. Large companies can also re-evaluate their advertising to maintain effectiveness and lower cost. It's all about how advertising relates to your sales dollar for dollar.

If sales and advertising are linked and measured, then keep doing up the programs providing the "cost per conversion" is traceable and makes sense. If not, then get out, pay your penalties and use the money in better ways...like paying your employees salary this week or the light bill. Even if cancellation fees apply, lights and salaries are higher priorities than advertising will ever be.

Normally you can break off contracts with media with little downside, but read the fine print. Consider asking for a 3-6 month hiatus from all promotion if cash is absent. Call the media outlets and ask for a "suspension" instead of a "cancellation". Cancellation might not allow you to recover the lower cost per insertion rates, whereas a suspension of the media might. It is a proven fact that in bad times, **companies who advertise effectively survive.** Those who withdraw completely, rarely do survive unless they have a long standing solid business base.

One last thought...that one time ad in a major media channel will not reverse declining sales. According to David Ogilvy the master of advertising, sustained advertising works best. He says if you can't do it all year, don't advertise. I think this is good advice. Perhaps you can lower your ad cost by changes in color, frequency or time. Once good times return, then advertise with gusto in proven channels which can be sustained.

Bankruptcy

Filing for Bankruptcy protection is a last resort for any business. In spite of what you hear, Bankruptcy is a wonderful way to get control of the business financially and work out a formal turn around and recovery plan, but it is not a panacea, nor is it a way to avoid paying off people you owe. Depending on how you file for bankruptcy protection, everyone will be paid either the full amount, a negotiated amount, or you will end up with nothing and they will get something.

One hidden secret to reckon with is that bankruptcy is not cheap. Last time I checked, hiring an accountant and a bankruptcy lawyer to oversee the bankruptcy process within their disciplines, filing fees and court costs totaled about $4,000.00 for a small firm and $50,000-$100,000 for a much larger one. Not cheep...and they will be paid first and upfront in most cases.

I hinted at the problem of delaying bankruptcy too long in a prior section. In this decision lies either spending many thousands needlessly, or saving those critical dollars to live another business day. I have seen it more times than not, that owners delay the ultimate filing far too long for it to be effective as a recovery enabler. Often the decision to file occurs **far later in time** then it ever should have.

If the business is on the decline and you can put your finger on the reason, and the reason is external to the business and not likely to change anytime soon...then send the people home with a good severance check, sell down the

assets, pay yourself back as best you can and file on the remaining bones if you have to. This statement answers the big question of "when should I file" bankruptcy. The second obvious question is "what Chapter should I use under U.S. Bankruptcy Law?"

Let's look at these questions. The first question bears on the decision of "when", not "how". That second question, (the how), should be between you and your attorney. I will point out though, that should you meet with a bankruptcy attorney – you need to bear in mind , that meeting is a legal event. You have just certified that the conditions within the firm are worthy of bankruptcy....so formally meet under extreme caution. This is all a creditor needs to show that your business is near, or at, insolvency.

You are really making a cascading decision. That decision flows down like this in my mind:

- ☐ I have a healthy and operating business
  - Nothing needed here, except expansion, refinement and efficiency improvements
- ☐ I need financial or business management help
  - You need outside help for sure and it can come from a best-practice coach
- ☐ I have serious financial losses and will turn around the business without filing for protection
  - Contact a "turn around consultant"
- ☐ **I have serious financial losses and will turn it around after filing**
  - **Chapter 11**
- ☐ **I will not turn it around and the business is insolvent**
  - **Chapter 7**

While I could break this down quite a bit more, these are the "big rocks in the jar" in the decision process as I see it. The last two in bold mark where some form of filing is required. Either Chapter 11 for protection and turnaround, or Chapter 7 for insolvency.

Side Bar

Is a bad business contract tearing your company down financially???

Consider Filing Chapter 11. Ask to be relieved of the contract and if approved, renegotiate the job and work the job under a new contract. It can be done.

No one wins in a bankruptcy...except perhaps the lawyers and accountants. Your suppliers loose, your bank creditors loose, your employees loose, shareholders loose, and most of all, you loose.

I am a firm believer that if the business model is sound, save the company. If the business model is under performing, change the business model, If the business model is bad, shut it down and start over with a new business model.

Part 1 - Last Thoughts

I am excited for you...you have a great start on understanding many of the dynamics of improving your business in a crisis cash situation. Before we leave Part 1, I am going to leave you with these last and important thoughts:

- With God's blessing, be in command of your destiny, don't let the external world control your attitude or your life.
- This is a crisis situation...form a sense of urgency.
- Stop spending cash, unless it makes or turns into immediate cash.
- If you want to save this business, get everyone involved.
- Be creative, now is not the time to be afraid of trying new things.
- Develop your data and refine your sources...the data needs to be highly accurate and timely.
- Take no excuses from producers of cash management data...hold the line on accountability for everyone...including you.
- Develop the Plan (work hardest here).
- Execute the Plan (work harder still).
- Make adjustments as needed as the Plan unfolds. Your Plan is a living information resource that needs in some cases, hourly revision.
- Continue the work after the crisis is abated.
- Just because things get better, don't stop managing your cash with a tight fist.

OK...so there it is...it's time to understand and develop your Crisis Cash Management Plan. In Part 2, we are going to accomplish the Plan step by step so relax, the fun of recovery is just beginning.

A final word of caution....Time is still not on your side, so take a break and then read on...your about two incredibly long and hard days from a measure of "cash certainty" and have accomplished one big critical step. That step has brought you closer to recovering your business through a better understanding of precisely how cash can be created and controlled in your struggling business.

PART 2

Crisis Cash Management Plan - Template

Part 2: Reading and Application Advice

If you have not read Part 1 completely, then go back and read Part 1 all the way through one time to gain an understanding of the various forms, information and mechanisms created within Part 2.

As you read this Plan-Template, some steps are presented in a "simple small business size format," which can be applied to almost any sized business. These concepts are easily scaled.

Where a Step needed more complexity to fully explain the concepts in larger business size, or where the concept would not scale well, I presented the step using a "complex project based business of multi-divisional size format."

Don't let the two formats confuse you because I am going to use both. The reason I use the two formats is that some steps would be very difficult to scale up in complexity from small business to large business format. However, it is relatively easy to digress (scale down) a larger format into a smaller sized business format. Understand the mechanisms first before jumping into the process.

Again, make sure information producers understand what they will contribute... as it bears heavily on the success of your end result. Speed and more importantly "accuracy" are essential as it costs money to be in business.

Remember, it does not matter what format you use to collect and record the data...it matters much more how accurate the information is and what you do with the data after it is collected and assessed.

Overview:

One picture is worth a thousand words...

Crisis Cash Management Plan

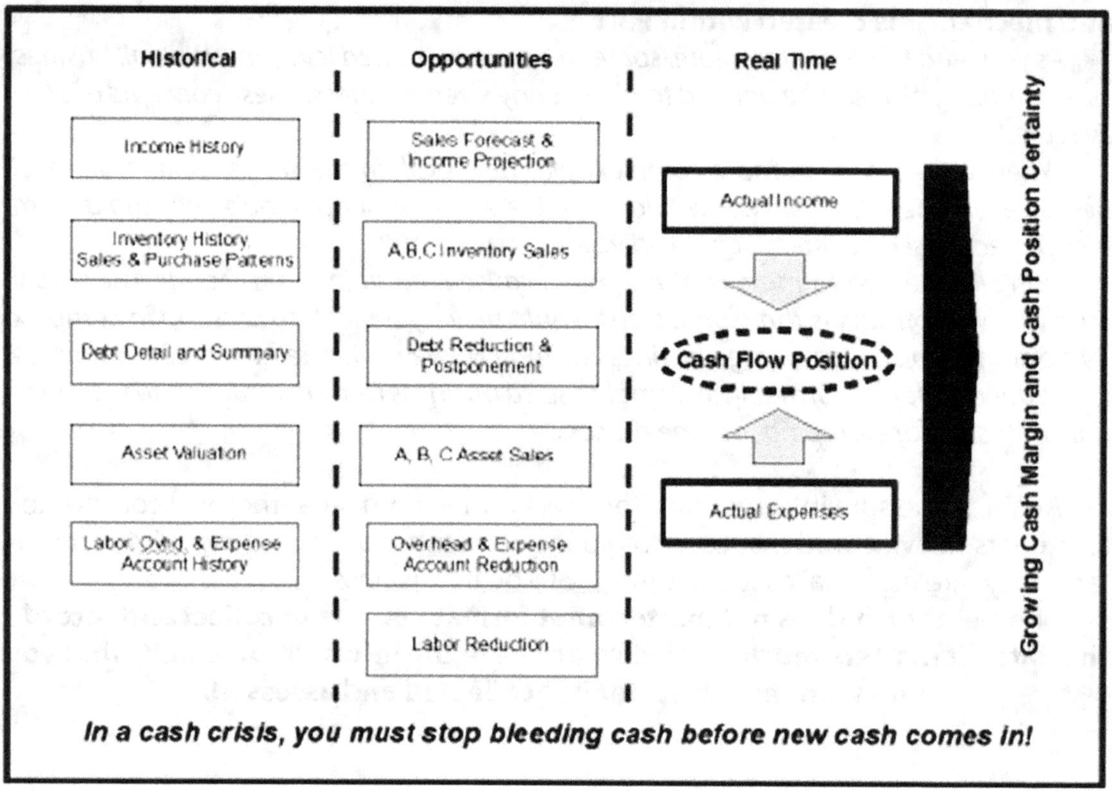

Why is the Plan a "Template"?

- It is a template because the final format of the business information is controlled solely by you.
- It is a template because it lacks your private business information.
- It is a template because generic spend and inflow categories need to be aligned to your specific business.

The **Crisis Cash Management Plan** is both a Template and a Process. It consists of several steps. Each step works with other steps to provide a controlled data collection, analysis and expanding view of cash certainty...and maybe even create a little reserve cash flow in the process when reductions are made and excess sales take place.

The Plan is divided into four (4) major Key Phases:

- **Phase 0:** Assembling the Team

- **Phase 1:** The **"Historical"** phase, gathers information about your company's activities, assets, inventory values and past sales history.
- **Phase 2:** The **"Opportunities"** phase, identifies sources of new cash both inside and outside the enterprise. It looks at ways to reduce the total outflow and increase inflow from the business.
- **Phase 3:** The **"Real Time"** phase is where Phases 1 and 2 come together and are applied to your company in "real time" for decision making support. It helps you analyze what is working and what is not working.

This Plan is only as good as the data used, commitment level, independent research and methods applied by you. You can accomplish some steps in an hour or two, some may take days, but unless the company is far out of control, most all can be accomplished in just a few days. The ultimate end product output is to create a Crisis Cash Plan that aids recovery using templates I have provided and/or those you create, each modified for your specific business.

It's your data, your categories of spend, your income...It's your business. If it's a cash crisis...then understand it, control it, and reverse it.

A word about data collection and form creation:

You are more than welcome to use the various samples provided in this book, or make up your own forms as needed to fit your business. I did not create them to be fool proof or dumb them down to be generic enough to fit all conditions. I created them to meet an objective of communicating an idea and a concept.

For those of you who want turn key solutions, there is several low cost software applications available on the Internet that will make the job of creating spreadsheets and entering data a bit easier, but it is not necessary if you have a working knowledge of basic spreadsheets and their functionality. I caution however, that in the past, I purchased and used one software application that will go unmentioned that was "locked" meaning that I had no control over the look or feel of the end documents. Control over the end product is something you need control over.

I have also produced all these documents, (the forms and financial "schedules"), by hand on ledger paper and it worked just fine as a process. Further, I also created the main Cash Flow Position ledger on a large black lined erasable white board. I used fine tape to set up the columns and grid. That single board became a visual plan for the troops to see and understand. Ultimately, because of its real time nature, it was a welcome vehicle to get behind the results. I like White Boards. They allow stakeholders to see the information visually. The troops need to see how they are progressing towards common goals. Along these lines, sometimes I create a "war room". A controlled access space where I lay out everything so I don't have to look for things in computers, drawers and file cabinets. Most times the walls "get papered" with "best available" information. I guess I am a visual kind of guy. But, for all its colorful nature, I could tell you in a few seconds what was happening in the firm and why without spending a lot of time switching views.

You will be creating a few simple Spreadsheets. These can be created in any routine spreadsheet software. In making your own forms, I recommend you use a simple spreadsheet format with separate columns which supports basic calculations. You will be adding, subtracting, multiplying and dividing. In some cases, you will be calculating ratios, so make sure you understand ratios and how to apply them within your program Plan.

OK you get the point....Let's Start Your Plan beginning with an overview of the phases and steps involved.

Plan Steps

(You might want to make a copy of this page and the Part 2 overview picture for distribution to your team and stakeholders.)

Now that you have a feel for the **Phases** involved in Part 2 as described in the beginning of this Part, let's review the specific steps under each Phase. The description below is very "high level" and details will be found under each Step Section in Part 2.

Phase 0:	Assemble the team and create a sense of urgency
Phase 1, Step 1:	Prepare an "Income History" for past 12 months (by business unit, customer, project and/or job)
Phase 1, Step 2:	Analyze inventory and purchase patterns (by SKU, category or vendor as required)
Phase 1, Step 3:	Debt Detail and Summary
Phase 1, Step 4:	Labor Review
Phase 1, Step 5:	Overhead Review
Phase 1, Step 6:	Direct Expense Review
Phase 1, Step 7:	Analyze individual expense account relationships to sales
Phase 2, Step 8:	Prepare an "Income Projection" using a "Sales Forecast"
Phase 2, Step 9:	Forecast cash outflow by project or business unit (including prioritizing as required)
Phase 2, Step 10:	A,B,C Inventory Sales
Phase 2, Step 11:	Reduce or Postpone Outstanding Debt
Phase 2, Step 12:	A,B,C Assets Sales
Phase 2, Step 13:	Overhead and Expense Account Reduction
Phase 2, Step 14:	Labor Reduction
Phase 3, Step 15:	Allocate cash in accordance with known budgets & priorities (customer, project or business unit)
Phase 3, Step 16:	Apply the work "real time"
Phase 3, Step 17:	Build a "cash cushion" using different means
Phase 3, Step 18:	Celebrate the victories

Phase 0: Assemble the team and create a sense of urgency

This important step lays the basic foundation for selecting, motivating and rewarding everyone in the business who will contribute towards the common goal... which I assume is "Reverse the critical cash crisis situation of declining cash flows to positive cash flows and net cash reserves".

I am going to use a bit of consultant speak here for a moment so just follow along as it will make sense in the end. I work using a RACI system taught to me by the consulting arm of KPMG[1]. I am including a form sample you can create which will define the roles of the parties and stakeholders in the Crisis Cash Management Plan. See the table below and make one for yourself with these headings. This really works to get everyone on the same page.

Decision Action Task	Responsible	Accountable	Consulted	Informed	Target Completion Date	Actual Completion Date

- The "Decision, Action or Task" is where you place the step, task and "need".
- The "Responsible" party is the person who will actually create or accomplish the task or item.
- The "Accountable" party is the person who is accountable for the performance of the responsible party.
- The "Consulted" party is the individual or group who need to be brought in to accomplish the mission.
- The "Informed" party is the person or persons who will be informed about the progress and will receive the results of the effort.
- "Target Completion Date" and "Actual Completion Date" columns are self-explanatory.

I have provided a working sample in this step detail below and also in Phase 2, Step 9 of several RACI forms in action. You can create one table per step, or one table for all steps. Initially, I would create one chart for the entire effort so people can see the entire list of steps and will know who is doing what function. Post your table/s on the wall big and large where everyone can see what's required and also issue it out as a formal document so they can refer to it frequently as they work the Plan. As the leader you will want a copy with you at all times so you can direct activity and know the points of interface, etc.

Let's drill this down into three key sub-steps of team creation.

Selecting People for the Core Team:

You will need each and all of the functions listed filled collectively or individually. In small companies, these functions can overlap well, but they must all be

1 "KPMG" is a registered trademark of KPMG International

performed. Do not start without having these functions in place and both their role in the recovery and their individual contribution carefully explained. This effort should take about one business day preceding the actual effort.

Crisis Cash Leader: The person accountable for the Crisis Cash Management initiative success or failure. Normally this is the owner of the business as they have the most riding on it's outcome, but it can also be the GM, CEO, Operations VP or other...even an outsider with proper authority to hire and fire. They must have the authority to make personnel changes as needed to execute the Plan. This person leads the effort...and will not direct someone to lead it for them. This is one time when you should not delegate the work if your life savings and work is on the line.

Crisis Cash Coordinator: This person coordinates all the information collected and used in the course of Crisis Cash Management. This central and pivotal role is more than an Administrator's function, this is someone who has the tenacity to motivate people to meet schedules, demand performance and steer involvement with the effort. It could be the bookkeeper, but I have found some of these types lack the will to go into direct conflict with perhaps Senior Management and Department Leaders when their performance is lacking. Part politician and part task master, next to the Leader this one position makes or breaks the performance of the effort. Better to be the Crisis Cash Leader, than let this function fail. One way to add power to the position is to use an "escalation system" where the Crisis Cash Leader is informed by the Coordinator whenever the planned dates are exceeded, or if personal issues arise.

Operations Team Member: Answers all questions about "when can we deliver products and services and issue the invoice" type questions. Normally this is a Senior Person in Operations who can see all the activities of "business value creation and delivery". Normally, installed departments like Operations Planning report to the Operations Team Leader during this initiative as they create the routine production and service planning schedules.

Sales Team Member: Answers all questions about sales forecasting and sales made. This is the lead negotiator for client relations...including sales of inventory and assets. Normally, it's a senior member of sales, such as a Sales Manager...but not always. You have to get this function right if you want any creditability of what the future holds.

Note: I caution putting too much burden on individual salesmen at this juncture. If it is a Crisis, pressure to produce more profitable sales is already occurring. They will be quite busy, (or at least they should be), just making new sales or finding out when a new sale is possible. If they are not performing these basis functions, the salesman is "extra baggage" and is not needed on the payroll. Shift them to pure commission. I don't want to thwart a salesman's success at the key task of selling. Salesmen should accomplish the main task of informing about new sales and forecasts in this process initiative, but we want them out selling...not spending a lot of time out of their prime function which is actually selling. Instead, I

would choose someone who works with Sales each day such as as a Sales Coordinator who knows the people and can coordinate information developed.
Bookkeeper/Accountant: Receives information from the Crisis Cash Coordinator to which they add the routine information they normally manage such as cash on hand, process receipts, interest, payables, etc. They can work closely with customers to escalate payments for sold goods and services. They can also work with suppliers and banks for payment delays.

Note: This position keeps the crisis cash management Cash Flow Position spreadsheet and data up to date in conjunction with Crisis Cash Coordinator input.
Let me say the above a different way. The Bookkeeper keeps the data of the Plan, disbursements and cash on hand values. The Crisis Cash Coordinator keeps the sales forecasts, production forecasts and income values current.
You may be wondering why the Coordinator and Bookkeeper functions do not just combine. Well they can...however, it is my experience that putting all this coordination and information on the bookkeeper, (in addition to dealing with normal creditors, bookkeeping duties, etc), causes them to buckle in a about a week. Plus, their personality is normally not of the "negotiator type". It's ultimately your call...but I would avoid overloading this position at all cost. Better to work this need yourself, than delegate the work and fail.
You may now have a cash flow program in place and this is great. For those of you lucky ones, I want to increase the information accuracy and increase the granularity of the data well beyond a monthly view. A monthly cash flow report is just not sufficient in a Crisis Cash Management scenario.

Extended Team

Others: Bank, Suppliers, etc. may not be on the core team, but should be on an "extended team" as indirect stakeholders of the business. I have also applied "external stakeholders on the Core Team with great success. You will need cooperation from all stakeholders in your recovery. I would involve them on the RACI Chart as needed, but if you do...have them (and the Core Team members) certify their role and accountability in writing using a brief letter agreement. Let's look at what one should look like.

Letters of Commitment:

The last thing you want is a failure of commitment just because it gets a little rough...and it will. Very rough indeed.
Consider supplying each core team member with a Letter of Commitment for their signature. The letter should document their role in the recovery and

each letter should have a place for the "core team member" to sign certifying their agreement. I have used these in the past and they tend to bind the individual to the cause in a formal manner. This way everyone is signed up and ready to operate. Below is a sample of one possible letter to learn the spirit of the Agreement. It makes an assumption that you have spoken to the individual about the mission and have confidence in their agreement to participate:

(For Core Team)
To: ______________________
Date: ______________________

The company (XYZ Company) has decided to prepare and execute a "Crisis Cash Management Initiative". This important initiative is designed to increase the information quality from all internal departments and external stakeholders with the specific goal of managing company resources and cash in an improved manner. The importance of this Initiative cannot be understated.
On ______________________ you agreed to join the "Core Team" of this initiative acting in the capacity of ______________________. Specifics of your responsibilities (are as follows 1,2 3...) <or> (will be discussed with you individually and collectively with the Core Team in the next 24 hours, whereas you will have the opportunity to withdraw your support of this Initiative).
Management understands this may/will place additional burdens on your current position and duties. However, we feel you have the skills and capacity to perform this temporary function without harm to your present work assignments, performance and responsibilities. Unless otherwise informed your current duties will remain. If, however, at any time you feel overwhelmed, or unable to perform the added responsibilities under this Initiative, you are directed to contact ______________ who will review the situation and make changes to the assignment as needed.
Again, this is a critical time for our company and we need the cooperation of everyone to meet the current challenges.
Welcome aboard the Crisis Cash Management Initiative "Core Team". Your signature below certifies your agreement to the above.

____

(Name)

____

(Signature, Date)

____

(Manager)

Sample RACI Chart for ALL Steps

Step	Task	Resp.	Acct.	Informed	Consulted
0	Team Dev.	L	L	CT	AR
1	Income Hist.	B	C	CT	L
2	Inv./Pur. Hist.	B	C	CT	L/ET
3	Debt Detail	B	C	CT	L/ET
4	Labor Review	O	C	CT	L/B
5	Ovh'd.	B	C	CT	AR
6	Expenses	B	C	CT	AR
7	Exp Accounts	B	L	L	AR
8	Income Proj.	S	L	CT	L/ET
9	Outflow Proj.	B	L	CT	AR
10	Inv. Sales	O	L	CT	S/L
11	Debt Change	L	L	CT	AR
12	Asset Sales	L	L	CT	S/O
13	Ovh'd Red.	O	L	AR	AR
14	Labor Cost	O	L	AR	B/C
15	Cash Alloc.	B	L	L	C
16	Application	CT	L	AR	L
17	Cash Cushion	CT	L	CT	AR
18	Celebrate	L	L	AR	AR

Key:
L = Leader,
C = Coordinator,
O = Operations,
S = Sales,
B = Bookkeeping,
CT = Core Team + L
ET = Extended Team
All = Core and Extended Team
AR = As Required

Phase 1, Step 1: Prepare an "Income History" for past 12 months

(By Business Unit, Customer, Project or Job)...whatever best defines your business income source flows.)

This information is historical in nature and allows you to validate "forward looking" Sales Forecast Projections, (made in a later step), to the same time frames from the previous year, SKU, customer, etc.

This work provides the means to look back at prior sales history, by Item (SKU), by Customer, Business Unit or Project so you can VALIDATE sales forecast assumptions. If done right, it will show trends in sales, (up or down), as well as capture any historical cycles found in the normal business revenue flow, e.g. seasonal sales. I recommend you use the same "time cycle format" you now use for your current Sales Forecast to simplify the comparison of income history to your forecast. If you can break it down further, then do so.

One possible output from this "multi view report" might be to prepare a column or two showing the "Percentage of line item income to total income in the same time period". We want to know where the bulk of our income is coming from as a percentage of sales. To accomplish this, just divide the line item total for the month (day, etc.) by the total income for the period, (month, day, etc.).

Note: This also works for SKU's and shows how these income producers are weighing in on total business revenue stream.

This effort focuses attention and recovery efforts on what is making the most income....meaning the line items that produce the bulk, (say 70-80%), of total revenue.

I have provided a sample spreadsheet format below you can use for this purpose. Just make sure the final form version allows you to at least accomplish the following:

1. A complete record of all revenue (income) by period
2. The lowest time granularity possible is better, but not greater than month to month
3. A way to sum income by time period
4. Sufficient granularity to compare income across multiple time periods
5. Relational percentages (such as "period to period") and ("item revenue to total revenue" for the given periods)

(Bold = Actual, Std. = Planned)	Example	Current Week	Week 1	Week 2
Cash Sales	100.00			
Credit Sales	100.00			
Interest	100.00			
Rentals	100.00			
Billed Sales	100.00			
Project 1	100.00			
Project 2	100.00			
Project 3	100.00			
Progress Payments	100.00			
Customer Advances	100.00			
Loans	100.00			
Rent or Rental Payments (cash In)	100.00			
Cash Sales	100.00			
Other Receipts	100.00			
Total Income	**1400.00**	**0.00**	**0.00**	**0.00**

(Example above does not show the column for line item percentage to total income)

You can create this information anyway you want, but I would make sure you have a reasonable way in which to look back over your income history and see where the funds are coming from at a very low level, when they occur, and if there is ground to use the data to validate a forward looking sales assumption or sales forecast.

Note: I did not show SKU's or Business Units, etc. on the above sample as they might confuse some people. I do know that most income data in a typical small to medium sized company lacks the level of detail we are after. Now in contrast, the detail might just be a click away through an ERP system, or other company wide software based management reporting system. Now would be a good time to discuss Report Writers.

Software based database "Report Writers"

Report Writers are a real Blessing.

Investigate what data you collect, how your data is stored in one or more databases, and if it can be accessed by a "report writer software" engine...even Excel. These tools allow you to "slice and dice" any accessible data to get to any search query or view needed. Once made, the report can repeat with a touch of a button.

I am not going to make firm application recommendations as the "flavors" are many, Just look up "report writer software" in an Internet search query and you will find some impressive applications that don't cost "an arm and a leg". You will come up with a fine list of software applications out there that work with almost any typical database application. Some offer free trial downloads for 30 days.

After years dealing with in IT, I have learned that "custom reports" written in direct computer language take a long time to get operational, are difficult to write in software languages like Basic and generally cost far more than a user's license for a good report writer which can be up and running in a day. Try to use "canned packages" for retrieving this data.

Phase 1, Step 2: Analyze inventory and purchase patterns (by SKU, category or vendor as required)

Here, we want to accomplish two major items.

- One effort will be to divide the inventory on hand into the three classes (A,B,C) previously defined in Part 1, the Crisis Cash Flow Guide and,
- Second, we want to see how inventory is actually being purchased over time, (and if possible, relate specific inventory items to future sales).

These two unique efforts allow organization of inventory into specific classes we can sell and also tie inventory to changes in sales forecast estimates. You will need this information to know what to sell off and what inventory is needed going forward as new sales occur. This highlights money you will spend later as sales are anticipated.

Class All Inventory: Follow directions in Part 1 for the Classification of Inventory. Basically, divide the inventory into the three classes mentioned, Class A, B and C. Do it by hand if necessary and make summary lists of each class in hard copy.

Determine Inventory Spend Over Time: Like the Historical Income Data, we need to understand the purchasing patterns of inventory over time...and if possible relate that view to future sales. It is likely you have this information either captured somewhere, or you have a good idea of how each item sells and when. All three Inventory Classes will be included in this analysis as it is historical. If Class B or C inventory was not included, it would distort the viewpoint.

We want to look at inventory in several ways. Make several columns to show all the data we need such as aggregate by month, by SKU and by Total Sales. Here are some possible guidelines to inventory analysis:

1. **Inventory turnover**. The number of times the inventory SKU is turning over for a given period...usually a business year. This view creates the classes of inventory A,B, C.
2. **Total inventory count of SKU's on hand by month.** This analysis shows how MANY inventory SKU's we have on hand month to month. We are interested in how the count changes over time and as we sell off unused inventory.
3. **Dollar value of a single SKU by month.** Stock values go up and down with seasons and sales activity. What we want to know is the change in dollars for a single SKU month to month. These variations can be related to our future sales providing the Sales Forcast is related by SKU.
4. **SKU total dollar value as a percentage of Total Sales**. Perhaps the most important analysis is this ranking of SKU's in dollars as a percentage of total sales. When percentages are sorted in descending order, we should have our top SKU seller first, second top seller second, and so on. These high valued items will need to be focused on first as they are the most expense to own and needed most. **Note:** If your using one or many inventory SKU's to make another SKU for ultimate sale, then this ranking will show what sells most, but will not show what

makes up the final SKU selling most. How they relate comes from a "Product Work Break Down" parts list, or equivalent. Record final assemblies and record how they sell. You will need to tie lower SKU's to the top SKU.

5. **Total inventory expenditures by month.** This view shows average cash outflow for inventory month by month. We need to understand how total inventory is varying month to month.
6. **Total sales by month, (does not includes sales of assets, etc).** This comparison shows how inventory changes by season and total sales dollars.

Remember, these outputs help us determine how inventory must adjust for changes in sales, e.g., if sales are going down, what inventory will be affected? If sales are going up, what do we need to have on hand in order to make money fast? This also answers where should we dump inventory and where should we replenish inventory to improve our recovery efforts?

We need a way to see all the relationships of inventory to our Sales Forecast. The easy way is when you have an Enterprise Resource Planning (ERP) or Demand Resource Planning (DRP) system. These tools allow for the projections of sales to flow directly to projected inventory needs if a Product Work Breakdown Structure exists in the system.

Our simple goal regardless of the method in a crisis of cash is to answer these questions:

"What do we need to have on hand that we can make money with...or are most likely to make money with?"

"What do we need to sell, locate, stock and use/deliver to earn money?"

What inventory can we sell?

This is just one view of the many we could create using a spreadsheet or reporting program.

Inventory History	(Bold = Actual, Std. = Planned)	Example	% of Sales	Current Month	Jan	Feb
Total Sales			**100.00**			
Purchase History	**SKU 1**	1.00	0.01			
Purchase History	**SKU 2**	2.00	0.02			
Purchase History	**SKU 3**	3.00	0.03			
Purchase History	**SKU 4**	4.00	0.04			
Purchase History	**SKU 5**	5.00	0.05			
Purchase History	**SKU 6**	6.00	0.06			
Purchase History	**SKU 7**	7.00	0.07			
Purchase History	**SKU 8**	8.00	0.08			
Purchase History	**SKU 9**	9.00	0.09			
Purchase History	**SKU 10**	10.00	0.10			
Purchase History	**SKU 11**	11.00	0.11			
Purchase History	**SKU 12**	12.00	0.12			
Purchase History	**SKU 13**	13.00	0.13			
Purchase History	**SKU 14**	14.00	0.14			
	Total Inventory Value	**105.00**		**0.00**	**0.00**	**0.00**

Phase 1, Step 3: Debt Detail and Summary

In Part 1, we looked at taking on additional debt as a source of additional funds and reconfiguring debt as a means of extending payments and boosting net cash flow margin. Let's look at them in detail, one by one.

1 **Credit Available:** Here, we need to know the sum and costs of all credit capacity remaining available under existing credit lines and show for each the rates of interest. I am not going to talk about obtaining new credit as this is a complete book in itself and the fact that new credit lines will normally be higher in cost than existing credit lines. Instead, I am looking for a summary schedule of credit money remaining available that can be leveraged to save the business.

1.1 Make a list of all credit facilities and record the cost of interest for each. **Every other means of cash creation through asset sales and liquidation of inventory should be exhausted before tapping high interest credit.**

1.1.1 You want to use the cheapest money first which means tap only those credit lines as required for immediate survival and only for a short time, say in the first week or month...beyond that time frame "you are spending your future."

1.2 Your personal wealth should never be put at risk. We covered use of credit in more detail in Part 1, so let me leave you with these final thoughts as I write this:

1.1.1 If personal signature guarantees are needed, you better be darnn sure you have a solid and tested plan for recovery. By "tested" I mean that you have worked the plan already and have high confidence in the results. Otherwise, consider selling or shutting the business down unless you are willing to risk it all.

1.1 Don't use high interest credit until absolutely necessary as high interest rate debt is very hard to pay off.

1.1.1 If you do use credit, have a plan to pay it back in one month or sooner. If available cash surfaces, pay down your credit lines quickly to reduce debt loads. Try sending in a separate check, (even for a small amount), noted as "additional payment towards loan principal". This will eat off the remaining balance faster than any routine debt payment made.

2 **Debt Reconfiguration:** Use "debt reconfiguration" as a means to both delay payment for a month or two and decrease interest rates when possible. Reconfiguring debt is a means to achieve lower payments, better terms, or forgiveness of debt. The last is possible, but depends on the relationship and many other factors including spend with the creditor if a supplier.

1.3 Lower payments raise the net cash flow margin by the value of the reduction. Every effort should be made to lower payments even if it is a small amount. This and other step outputs may add up to positive cash flow under the toughest times.

1.4 Moving payments to the end of the operating note is a great way to buy some cash flow margin and may be a first strategy with many secured creditors. Try to move not less than three months of payments to the end of the note. That will buy you some serious time to sort things out in initial recovery. If you fail at three, try for two or even one payment shift to the end of the note. This one time boost may be the difference of whether the company has the funds to make payroll or buy critical items for making new cash.

1.5 Lowering interest rates is a great way of lowering payments. Most banks and creditors will not adjust rates without cause, but I would try anyway... especially if you were current up to this point. You might squeeze out a half point or two with a refinance of existing debt. This is a great target when rates have shifted substantially lower and credit is abundant. Move any remaining debt to a new lending source if the current creditor does not budge and the rates are attractive. You will have options here and should use them all.

2 **Debt reconfiguration will boost your cash margins dollar for dollar.**

2.1 I once investigated swapping debt for equity (stock) in a large company. On face value it is easy. In practice however, it was extremely complicated and required a lawyer who made $500 an hour just to draft the agreements. It can be done, and is being done more and more....just ask GM. Be mindful that debt swaps require several key ingredients:

2.1.1 Holders of existing debt who are willing to trade a good bankruptcy position "trades payable" to a lesser position "preferred stock". This swap usually moves debt to equity and moves the debtor to a stockholder. Stockholders are behind trades payable in class of debt at bankruptcy. Therefore the swap has to be good for them financially and they usually require a high degree of trust in the turn around.

2.1.2 Legal vehicle to exchange debt for stock.

2.1.3 Time to pull it all together. This is quick to do in theory and long in time to execute...especially if it is a public company. SEC approval is normally required for the public company.

2.1.4 Stockholders who are willing to accept the change in company stock issues and its possible change in valuation.

Phase 1, Step 4: Labor Review

All labor used in making or delivering value to a customer or end user are direct employees. All other labor is indirect.

In this step we need to review your entire indirect and direct labor profile to understand how direct and indirect employees and revenue relate one to another. Here is one method to get to the answers needed. The end goal is three basic outputs:

1. What is the profile of labor?
2. What is the relationship of Labor to Revenue?
3. What is the sensitivity of Labor by skill to varying revenues historically earned?

To achieve these answers, you can follow the method below or use your own methods.

1 **Output #1.** Prepare a list, (a schedule), of all labor and show name, employee number, whether direct or indirect, department, skill, title, pay per period, annual salary and start date.

2 **Output #1.** Sort labor by the pay received for a given (same) pay period in descending order. This ranks all employees, highest paid on top.

3 **Output #1.** Determine the ratio of direct to indirect using pay and head count for each month over the past 12 months. This gives you some indication of whether the head counts are artificially increasing and whether pay has ballooned in one or more classes of employee.

4 **Output #2.** Break out the "Income History" (IH) report prepared in Phase 1, Step 1. For the same year and time span, look at your year end financials for Total Labor contribution as a percentage of COGS. Compare these annual numbers report to report. They should be the same. If not, reconcile the numbers.

5 **Output #2.** Match time periods of Income History to Labor Report month to month. This forms a "time based relationship" of direct and indirect labor to the IH report. What we want to know is how much labor in people count and dollars were consumed to achieve the sales recorded for any given period. These results give you:

5.1 Number of Direct Employees (count) to Revenue by period
5.2 Number of Indirect Employees (count) to Revenue by period
5.3 Total Direct Labor dollars to Revenue by period
5.4 Total Indirect Labor dollars to Revenue by period
5.5 **Note:** If you can break labor down even further to Customer, SKU or other metric then do so on a separate sheet, but use the same time base.

6 **Output #3.** Prepare a month to month comparison of the information in Point 5 above. This will show you how flexible direct and indirect labor is to achieve revenue. The greater the percentage, the less sensitive labor is to achieving a given revenue.

6.1 *This relationship is important as it gives you the first, and strongest, aggregate look at how sensitive labor is to revenue.* e.g. If the percentage is say 10% variable "peek to valley", then you can relieve 10% of Labor without overly burdening Labor. If 30%, than 30% can be relieved and so on.

6.2 **My caution is not to arbitrarily apply unilateral labor reduction factors to answer real world needs.** Instead, this study is a quick means to "work top down on a bottom up problem". The question being..."how much labor do we really need to achieve the current and future sales we anticipate"? In my mind, that last question can only be solved by relating actual sales, (and thus "production requirements"), to available labor...skill by skill, body by body.

7 With the above, we have accomplished our three outputs and perhaps more. This was a get ready step. In a later step, we will be making the hard decisions about RIF using in part this data.

Phase 1, Step 5: Overhead Review

Overhead is that portion of total enterprise disbursements used in the basic operation of the company. These are not expenses normally found in Cost of Sales which includes direct labor, materials and factory overhead. These are a host of item expenses that help the company function.

Here is a list of possible Overhead expenses to consider as a portion of total expenses:

- Indirect labor
- Labor benefits
- Retirement
- Management incentives
- Supplies
- Taxes
- Insurance
- Rentals
- Depreciation
- Utilities
- Telephone/Internet
- Travel
- Outside Services
- Entertainment
- Dues and Donations
- Advertising
- Sales Commissions

Overhead is often the first target of cost reduction strategies as it is not directly tied to the production of goods or the delivery of services. One can see from the list above that each cost should be a target for reduction...if not elimination.

1. For each item above determine the expense per month and the ratio of the individual expense to total expenses, (total outflow).
2. Rank them by order of magnitude in descending order
3. Starting at the top, find a means to decrease each one. Every dollar saved is a positive dollar to the Cash Flow Position.
4. The basic objectives are:
    1. Elimination of the expense
    2. Reduction of the expense
    3. Postponement of the expense

In all my work in cash flow and cost reduction, I have never had a single occasion where I could not find significant money in Overhead avoidance and reductions to add back to the net cash flow position.

Of course some expenses will be required in each active category no matter what...as the business must continue to function. However, by carefully studying each ratio of the individual expense to total expense and the contribution of that expense to earning revenue, one can get a strong feeling of what can be eliminated, what can be substantially reduced, and what can be postponed...and for how long. Do not give up until you have rung out every dollar in this category. Make the core team responsible for finding the fat and trimming it away.

Fact: If you cut off all expenses unless approved in writing, (even for small purchases), you will quickly learn what is a "must have item" and what is a "should have" or "like to have" item. ***Further, you will be amazed at how creatively some expenses are justified as "must have items"!***

Fact: You must control and modify a culture by those who have not had to deal with the absence of cash of spending company money without forethought...Go Lean.

Phase 1, Step 6: Direct Expense Review

(Direct Labor is covered in Step #4)

Here we want to look at all "direct expenses" in relation to total and individual item and service revenue. This will help us analyze how these direct costs are being applied for each sales dollar earned. Be mindful of large infrequent or one time expenses that will distort the numbers. Justify out each large one time expense or factor infrequent expenses in as an additional COGS burden.

1 Compute direct expense to total revenue as a ratio (percentage) for each item by month. Total and plot the results.

1.1 This shows how direct expenses vary as a percentage of revenue. The greater the variance the less sensitive the earning of revenue is on direct expense.

2 Determine COGS for each item or service as a percentage of individual product or service revenue. Sort list in descending order, highest percentage on top.

2.1 This sort shows where the company is spending the most of its money trading "red ones for blue ones". (Please go back and read Part 1 on making "profitable sales" if you are confused.) Consider eliminating (or postponing) the highest 20% of the list. In a cash crisis, why take on all the risk of producing and delivery if the sale has the highest COGS per revenue dollar...and thus lowest gross margin. Better to consolidate your activities to the items and services which really make money.

2.2 Case in point. Recently, someone came up to me that had a small repair business. Times were a bit rough so they took on work just to have cash coming in, even though it was not really very profitable. Well you guessed it...they ran into difficulty delivering on their repair commitments and it cost them heavily to finish the work. Now weeks later, out of money and out of options they are in deep trouble. The cash received by "selling at any cost" bought them some time, but created a deeper crisis downstream by reduction of their ending cash position.

2.3 While I am on profitable sales, in a real crisis, you can forget about maintaining "brand image" and the like. Your brand image...while important, essential and has a perceived value...will only have a real cash value if the company remains alive to leverage that brand. Better to make temporary adjustments that keep the firm alive until such time as the company can overhaul its low sales margin.

2.4 **Focus on what makes money first and the rest will follow.**

3 The number of direct expense possibilities are endless, so I am going to generalize a bit by forcing them into the more common buckets and provide some guidance on what is possible for each type of spend:

1.1 **Tools and Equipment (not Vehicles)**

1.1.1 Keep what you need. Sell off the rest.

1.1.2 Rent what you use infrequently or cannot afford to own outright.

1.2 **Raw Materials**

1.2.1 If you bought low, sell some of them off (say 30-50%) to build some reserve cash. Better to "profit this up" so to speak, than hold on to them and hope for a brighter day through consuming them.

1.2.2 If you bought high, sell some so you can recapture the cash they represent. You need the liquid cash and markets might be falling, so get out of the inventory position quickly.

1.2.3 Leverage long term low price agreements when possible by converting them to spot by selling off the long term position. You can always readjust to the new cost structure, unless the position IS your competitive advantage. If it is, then your business model is a "buy low-sell high" model and is predicated on your ability to buy low and sell high...what if there are no buyers tomorrow or next week at your price. Still want the raw materials... or the liquid cash???

1.3 **Purchased Parts and Assemblies**

1.3.1 A really tough one to call out basics on. I think this is an "informed gut call" and has to be based on specific forecasts of sales, and the belief in the company's ability to convert those parts and assemblies to sales gross profit. Here again...spending 94-96 cents and risking a lot just to make 4 cents.

1.3.2 In a crisis, these are the worst items to sell off because of their inherent custom nature. I would instead, tighten this up to only high active inventory in turns. If I need to stock items to sell items, then match all inventory spend to sales, dollar for dollar.

1.4 **Outside Purchased Services**

1.4.1 Eliminate the service. Most services not directly tied to making money can be eliminated.

1.4.2 Start doing it yourself internally. We did this at one company with great success. Help keep the dollars flowing to our people, instead of outsiders.

1.4.3 Find lower cost services. There is always someone willing to do it cheaper, but you still must balance risk and performance.

1.4.4 Charge the customer for the service directly in some way. If the customer is the beneficiary, then find a way for them to pay for it...or elect to opt out.

1.5 **Factory Overhead**

1.5.1 I define this category as all the indirect overhead expenses the factory needs to operate.

1.5.2 Defer maintenance only after a Job Risk Analysis is done sighting how long the maintenance can be deferred before issues develop. You must know what to watch out for to know to know when the item is failing, how the condition will be monitored, and by whom.

1.5.3 A typical factory can get by on less...but not for long. You need to review every item in the factory overhead list and make **team decisions** of what can be eliminated, deferred or engineered out of the cost equation. The CPR form in a later step will help determine this.

1.6 **Vehicles**

1.6.1 Have employees use their own cars instead of company cars.

1.6.2 Sell underutilized trucks and cars off and lease them back at a reduced rate. Take the cash from the sale and save the company.

1.6.3 Look for deals where you reduce cost of ownership substantially. I buy Government vehicles on some occasions....low cost, well maintained and in total life cycle costs to me...cheap to operate.

1.6.4 Make a list, (including your own cars paid by the company), trim off 20% and then trim it again by 20%. You are likely now at the leanest you can operate at.

1.6.5 Share rides and share operation. Use public transportation. Get smarter.

1.6.6 Defer maintenance for a quarter. Make good repair/replace decisions based on cash flow, not wants or desires.

Phase 1, Step 7: Analyze individual expense account relationships to sales

The information produced in this step helps us tie Expense Accounts to Sales. I am having you look at this account in such a way as to determine if a relationship between sales and expense accounts exists...and to what degree.

If sales are declining, we need to stop or set hard limits on expense account spend. I say simply stop all expenditures that are not ***directly tied to a given sale***.

In theory, expense accounts are not tied directly to sales, "dollar for dollar". True, expense accounts are hard to justify to actual sales income. Often expense accounts have little, if any, bearing on actual sales.

There are always ways to improve customer contact without incurring individual expense account burden. By being creative using Internet based meetings and other non-physical communication techniques, we can save big money. We can always sell more with same or less expenses. Again, please refer to Part 1 for more info.

"I suggest that until you get a handle on net cash outflow and end cash is rising, stop this incredibly wasteful outflow, unless it is directly tied to creating an order or making immediate cash."

Expense Account	(Bold = Actual, Std. = Planned)	Example	Current Month	Jan	Feb	Mar
Expense Account	John	100.00				
Expense Account	Sally	100.00				
Expense Account	Greg	100.00				
Expense Account	Sue	100.00				
	Total Expenses	400.00	0.00	0.00	0.00	0.00

Normally, I just say stop all expense accounts until further notice, or place it on a CPR form, (CPR's are discussed in Step 5 below). Please also refer to Part 1 for more advice on this issue.

During crisis cash management allow only those direct expenses which are tied directly to making money.

Phase 2, Step 8: Prepare an Income Projection using a "Sales Forecast"

Most companies use some form of a **Sales Forecast**. If not, you can use the example below to prepare a simple Sales Forecast.

This document provides a future horizon of what kinds of sales should be coming in the near term and beyond. **What we need to know most is the expected amount of gross income we will receive and the date we expect the money to arrive.** This needed information, in conjunction with the outputs of other steps will ensure you do not spend more cash then you actually expect to take in. If you use a Formal Sales Forecast, it will provide the information needed. If not, then make a schedule using the sample format shown below or something similar.

Your Sales Forecast should list all the sales the company anticipates making using a very granular time horizon. It provides a "forward looking" projection of sales with the closest time to the present divided into smaller units of time...say days initially, then weeks, and finally months in that order. We want to see the future sales horizon using a finite time system such as the following:

- By Days for 30 (or even 60) days out.
- By Weeks for 3 months after the initial period of 30 or 60 days.
- By Months beyond...optimally, we want a one year sales horizon...but longer is really nice if the sales are consistent and interruptions in sales small.
- Project based income is recorded as all planned payment milestones minor or major.

The key objective here is to gain a realistic and accurate sales forecast of income....projected out as far as possible

Create your income projection spreadsheet as shown below. Enter your data as required from your Sales Forecast. We are going to use this information shortly.

Sales Forecast	(Bold = Actual, Std. = Planned)	Example	Day 1	Day 2	Day 3
Forecast	***Project 1***	100.00			
Forecast	***Project 2***	100.00			
Forecast	***Project 3***	100.00			
Forecast	***Project 4***	100.00			
Forecast	***Customer 1***	100.00			
Forecast	***Customer 2***	100.00			
Forecast	***Customer 3***	100.00			
Forecast	***Customer 4***	100.00			
Forecast	***Customer 5***	100.00			
Forecast	***Customer 6***	100.00			
Forecast	***Customer 7***	100.00			
Forecast	***Customer 8***	100.00			
Forecast	***Customer 9***	100.00			
Forecast	***Customer 10***	100.00			
	Total Forecast Sales	**1400.00**	**0.00**	**0.00**	**0.00**

Crisis Cash Management in a "Project Environment":

I am going to detour a bit here into projects for those companies who are project based. Projects are quite a bit different than routine OTC sales, wholesale, or sales of products and services through other means including the Internet.

Most projects have a beginning, a middle, and an end, however some projects seem to go on forever.

It is fairly easy to have a project start out making money and then "lose the rabbit of profitability" as I call it. Some don't even know they've lost the rabbit until the last bill is paid.

In modest to large projects, (say types like "make to order', "engineer to order", etc.), Crisis Cash Management takes on a completely different tone. In a decline, Projects suffer from the lack of cash. Cash for expenditures and finally income (progress payments in most cases), are held up because of incomplete work fueled by lack of available funds. If you can't pay for the items you need to complete a phase, you can't collect progress payments....it's as simple as that.

Projects at a deeper level

By their very nature, Projects require that different people be responsible for different components of the project. Income streams are overseen by usually a project coordinator or manager. The time horizon of the project is finite and therefore requires oversight by a specific manager working within a defined operating and oversight authority. Contributors inside and outside the business make the project happen. Project costs are handled by internal cost centers, overseen by the Project Manager. .

Projects also depend on both vertical and horizontal business functions. Projects are typically vertical profit centers within a business unit or company that "consume" horizontal corporate resources. Those resources can including labor, facilities and inventory SKU's that might cross several projects. Some of these hard assets, (if not all), will survive the project to work another day on a different project. All this, to create basically a one time profit stream which will ultimately end by design...or by force.

Beyond the individual business unit project model, a project might also consume "shared services" in the form of corporate management support, central purchasing, IT and the like. That overhead also must find its way into the Profit and Loss of the project and the business unit that consumed it.

One way is to use apportioned cost. This can be done any number of ways. I like the simplicity of adding a burden percentage based on historical shared service overhead but prefer to record these as Activity Based Costs (ABC) so direct costs are allocated in proportion to the services received. Easy to say...hard to map and record. Stick with percentages if you lack a ABC structure.

Routinely, Income and expenses on the project cash flow sheets vary from the income and expenses of the business unit cash flow sheets. Each must roll up to the corporate cash flow sheet where decisions are made on allocations of resources. To meet this critical need, we must organize our cash flow sheets individually for this purpose in such a way as to allow easy summation at a higher level.

When cash is tight, priorities must be balanced between the needs of the project and the needs of the business unit supporting the project. That balance is critical to the further creation of corporate wealth....income.

Projects: Income Projection

(By customer, month, project, or job):

In a project environment, income must be projected and managed in real time as the project progresses.

When I managed large and medium projects, I used "S Curves" to visually see how the project was progressing to income projections and to predetermined expense budgets. I also used traditional cash flow sheets to monitor "plan to actual" which accounted for both income and expenses. These tools allow me to see the progress and deviations early enough to make required changes. In a declining cash position, most Project Managers do not know the project is overrunning expenses until it is too late. Early warnings allow for easy minor corrections to get the project back on track.

Deviations in Project expense are a direct loss of net profit, dollar for dollar.

In projects, income (revenue), comes in the form of progress payments received for work performed and also for related sold goods and/or services. Obviously, this is "new cash blood" coming into the company that provides for payroll, supplier payments for materials and services, overhead payments and all the countless other expenses incurred in the normal course of executing a project in a business. Cash remaining after subtraction of all expenses is "gross profit". Gross profit can be large, small, or even negative in value. Monitoring the work to achieve progress payments then is key to obtaining planned income on time...or earlier if possible.

As we look at project income side, I have prepared below some thoughts:

- The Project Manager is ultimately responsible for the combined cash flow of any project under his assigned control. This is the management of both the income and outflow of the project and the dates of those events.
- Cash flow income projections normally cover the "project time line in its entirety."
- This is an example where the P&L of the project is within the business unit. Project Income Projections are rolled up into the Business Unit Income Projection Schedule.

Business Unit Income Projections	
Project -1 Income Projections	Project -2 Income Projections

Note: I should add that when business units do not record the P&L of the project, P&L of the project bypasses the business unit financials and is recorded at the corporate level. In this case, the business unit effort is part of COGS in the project financials and the business unit receives a credit for creation of project. Bottom line is that it doesn't matter how profit and costs are recognized so long as it is visible, meets GAAP and is documented. Not all projects are profitable and not all projects are designed to create a profit.

- We must see the entire project time line both for income and for expense. Payment milestones must be accurate and realistic. Being conservative is important when we desire a positive cash flow position throughout the project time line. This means the company should normally not finance the project, unless it assumes this role and is paid for the service. Optimally, we want to be "working on the customers money" through the entire project or slightly behind. Down payments without value creation are hard to collect on, but a small commitment payment can usually be obtained. It is less risk if we do not need to borrow money to make money.
- Constant verification of the immediate income horizon (say out one or two quarters), must be done daily by the Project Manager to avoid financial surprises. Important large milestone payments must be managed for time and value from the onset of the project.
- Income Projections must be accurate and adjusted as often as required to reflect real time changes in contract performance and income. Change orders are a good example of when such adjustments are needed. So are incentives tied to early performance.

Let's shift gears to look at roles in a project environment as roles lead our way of thinking. For projects, it is usually the Project Manager who must manage the project's cash flow...including income and expense projections. For Business Units supporting the Project, it is the Business Unit Manager who must manage the profit and loss of his or her Business Unit. Combined, these two distinct parts of the cash management team are dependent on each other for mutual profit and loss. Most always, their objectives align, but sometimes they are at odds in terms of cash flow and setting priorities for cash resources when cash is limited. Therefore, we need a more global cash allocation process. **The following roles and responsibilities will give you more indication of who is responsible for what activities in the project income projection process.**

Task	Operating Level	Responsible	Accountable	Informed
Develop and maintain project cash income projections	Project	Program Manager	Operations Manager	Business Unit Manager
Integrate project income projections into business unit income projections	Business Unit	Business Unit Integrator	Business Unit Manager	Business Unit Manager
Integrate business unit cash projections by project into division income projections	Division	Division Priority Integrator	Division President	
Integrate division cash projections into corporate income projections	Corporate	Corporate Comptroller	CFO	CEO

The above is but one of many possible role selections in cash flow income collection and control. For our purposes here, we will follow this line as the above is a proven system tested under fire after billions of dollars of projects. Again, I am presenting this information for a complex project in a multi-divisional company so you can scale it back to your company size and complexity of financials.

Phase 2, Step 9: Forecast cash outflow by project or business unit (including prioritizing as required)

Depending on the circumstances involved, typically we can say that there are three different inputs when forecasting total cash outflow. The three (3) main outflows are:

Projected Cash Requirements (A)	Fixed Cash Requirements (B)	Unanticipated Cash Needs (C)

Let's look at each one as they have unique features and requirements.

A) Projected Cash Requirements (including prioritizing those requirements):

Projections are project, job or business unit specific and should encompass at least a sixteen (16) week projection. Longer projections add value to the "cash need horizon." This is specifically true where large cash needs can be mapped, such as in capitol improvement projects or very large expenses.

Prioritizing cash outlays improve the effectiveness of the cash allocation process. Prioritizing should be performed for the project, the job, and the business unit. The following table shows the person and/or groups responsible for carrying out the process steps for Projecting Cash Requirements under the tasks shown in the table below.

Again, we are using a large project environment so you can see a complicated framework. If you can understand this complexity level, then you can understand the simpler cash outflow model and how it would relate to your business.

Example of one possible Project Outflow tool:

Stage	Priority	# Item	PO #	PO Date	Vendor	Total PO $	Open $	WK1		
								Planned	Allocated	Actual
Planed	1	101	NA	NA	Steel	1,200,000	0	200,000		
Actual	2	101	P1054	3-12-01	North Star	1,160,000	1,000,000	160,000	160,000	160,000
Planed	PM	PM	PM	PM	PM	PM	PM	PM	blank	blank
Actual	PM/Ops	PM	PUR	PUR	PUR	PUR	ACCT	PM	CORP	ACCT

Above, we are looking at a budget that ultimately becomes a firm commitment of spend in the form of a Purchase Order. Note the "Planned", "Allocated" and "Actual" columns. Introduction of "allocated" as a column allows a record that the cash outflow has been approved and is timed to the expected issue date. The column on "Priority" is an internal tracking system designed to sort the most important (critical) outflows. We want to know where the greatest corporate or project risk exist should we miss the date of disbursement. The variations on this are endless, but you get the objective.."knowing projected cash outflow requirements".

The following roles and responsibilities will give you more indication of who should be responsible for which activities under Projected Cash Requirements.

Task	Operating Level	Responsible	Accountable	Informed
Develop and maintain 16 week project cash projections/assign project level cash priorities	Project	Program Manager	Business Unit Operations Manager	Business Unit Operations Manager
Integrate project cash projections by priority into business unit priorities	Business Unit	Business Unit Priority Integrator	Business Unit Manager	Business Unit Manager
Decide business unit priorities	Business Unit	Business Unit Manager	Division President	Division Priority Integrator, Senior Div. Operations Mgr.
Integrate business unit cash projections by priority into division priorities	Division	Division Priority Integrator	Division President	
Decide division cash priorities	Division	Senior Div. Operations Mgr.	Division President	Division President Corporate Cash Manager, VP Materials
Integrate division cash projections by priority	Corporate	Corporate Comptroller	CFO	

In a simpler company, the cash outflow projections can follow a simple "what we plan to spend and when" format.

B) Fixed Cash Requirements (Allocations)

As the term implies, a fixed cash budget is "allocated" on the basis of projected requirements and past history. Fixed allocations can occur at any level, such as a business unit, division or at a corporate level. Dollars are requested, approved and allocated over the same time period as Projected Cash Outflow. Fixed Allocation places certain amounts of re-occurring budgets aside for the Business Unit's specific use in a defined area of spend, but not at the detail level.

An example might be MRO and services that sustain the business unit operation. It needs a cash budget allocation a business unit can use as it sees fit and distribute through local purchase orders to vendors. Vendor payments for these types of purchase orders is insured...as a cash allocation has been set aside and a budget has been established and distributed.

Allocation Budgets normally are not adjusted upward without the approval of the (Owner, Assigned Manager, Comptroller). Someone of authority must approve any purchase that exceeds the budget allocation or is greater than (say 10%) of the total monthly allocation.

Note: Don't get overwhelmed because you are looking at a model of a large company's process. The main thing you must understand here is that there is a formal approval process which applies to any event which exceeds a baseline allocation budget and the setting of cash outflow priorities.

Here is one process for identifying and distributing a fixed budget in a large firm:

Task Sequence	Operating Level	Responsible	Accountable	Informed
Develop history of past spend in the subject area of focus.	Business Unit	Accounting	Division Comptroller	Business Unit Manager
Develop cash projection of business unit priorities	Business Unit	Assigned Task by Business Unit Manager	Business Unit Manager	
Decide business unit priorities	Business Unit	Business Unit Manager	Division President	Priority Integrator Senior Div. Operations Mgr.
Integrate business unit projections by priority into division priorities	Division	Division Priority Integrator	Division President	
Decide division cash priorities	Division	Senior Div. Operations Mgr.	Division President	Division President Corporate Cash Manager, VP Materials
Integrate corporate cash projections by priority	Corporate	Corporate Comptroller	CFO	
Allocate Fixed Budgets	Corporate	CFO	CEO	Division Comptroller, Business Unit Manager
Distribute Allocated Fixed Budgets	Business Unit	Division Priority Integrator	Division Operations	BU Accounts Payable, BU Manager, BU Purchasing Manager
Apply (Commit) Fixed Budgets - Overhead Materials and Services	Business Unit	Yard or Business Unit Manager to Purchasing Manager	Division Operations	BU Manager, BU Purchasing Manager
Apply (Commit) Fixed Budgets - Job Direct	Business Unit	Purchasing Manager	Division Operations	BU Manager, BU Purchasing Manager

C) Cash allocation for unanticipated priorities

A Business must reserve a measure of cash for handling unanticipated expenditures, as all cash needs will not be planned. Reactive cash needs grow in direct proportion to the error of the Projected Cash Plan and Fixed Cash Plan. Let me say this again, as it is critically important you understand this.

The more accurate you are in planning your cash outflows...the less reactive cash is needed and thus less drama is created.

The allocation and distribution procedure for unanticipated cash is the same for projected and fixed allocations. The reactive portion of the plan consists of capturing unanticipated or immediate cash needs that were not projected or fixed at the project level, or as part of a business unit's normal cash projections.

CPR Form:

The form below named "Cash Priority Request" or (**CPR**) was developed by me to aid in managing this process. **Note:** If the CPR form is used, AND the cash need exists on the "projected" cash sheet normally rolled up from the project, business unit, division or corporate, the projected or fixed schedules must be changed for the affected time period.

The CPR form, by its very nature, acknowledges the cash need is a HIGH priority of request. Time for decision and recommendations are all part of the data entered on the CPR form. Allocation of cash under a CPR format should be minimized at all times. Causes of failure in planning for CPR needed cash through Projected or Fixed Budgets should be investigated and resolved thus reducing the need for the forms use.

(Please look at the "Cash Priority Request" attached for detailed arrangement of fields and information required by the submitter.) Forms may be sent electronically by email or via fax to the respective party such as the Crisis Cash Coordinator for processing. The process below is one way to handle and process approvals.

(Complex Project Based Company)

Number	Process Steps	Responsible
1	Requisitioner Completes CPR Form with required data to establish priority and impact	Requisitioner
2	Business Unit Manager approves all Business Unit Requests (and)	Business Unit Manager
3	Division Operations Manager approves all Business Unit Requests (or)	Division Operations Manager
4	Division President approves all Business Unit and Division Requests (or)	Division President
5	Division CPR Administrative Coordinator processes request to Corporate Controller	Division CPR Administrative Coordinator
6	Corporate Controller Allocates Priority Funds (or) notifies Division Administrator of problems including any timing of funds to meet the desired request	Corporate Controller
7	Division Administrator informs all parties of status and/or coordinates changes as required	Division Administrator
8	Corporate Controller informs all parties and closes the CPR when payment is made. The form stays open until either the requisitioner withdraws it or it is approved and paid.	Corporate Controller

(Simple Company)

(Simple Company)

Number	Process Steps
1	Requisitioner Completes CPR Form with required data to establish priority and impact
2	Request is logged and processed by Crisis Cash Coordinator, CPR routed to Owner/Manager for approval.
3	Owner/Manager solicits information (as needed) and makes decision on request. The form stays open until either the requisitioner withdraws it or it is approved and paid.
4	If approved, bookkeeper allocates Priority Funds (or) notifies Owner/Manager of problems including any timing of funds to meet the desired request
5	When payment is made, Crisis Cash Coordinator informs all parties of funding and closes the CPR

I cannot emphasize enough that the CPR form is a "short circuit" and "pressure relief valve" of the true cash outflow process. People will find it is easier to use a CPR then to plan cash outflow correctly. Abuse of the CPR system only leads to more chaos and higher emotional drama in the business as the percentage of CPR cash increases.

Cash Priority Request (CPR) **(Data is entered in gray fields)**

Requester:	Date:	Tracking Control Number:
Business Unit:	Week Number:	1

Define the "Cash Priority" needing resolution:	State $ Amount Requested *(Only what's needed at the time needed)* $	Priority: Stops Production ☒ Delays Schedule ☐ Maintains Schedule ☐
Define the potential "Impact" to the company in terms of time, cost, personnel, and/or risk:		
Describe the best negotiated solution from your perspective:		
Enter the Hours or Days available to make the decision before the impact described above becomes a reality.		

When is a response needed? Date:
Describe the downside risk for taking no action on this cash priority request:
Enter below the desired steps necessary for resolution:

Action:		Accountable Party:	Needed Completion Date:	Agreed MGMT
1				☐
2				☐
3				☐
4				☐
5				☐
6				☐

Final Management Decision/Modification:

Decision-Maker: (enter initials)

Phase 2, Step 10: A,B,C Inventory Sales

In Phase 1, Step 2, we divided inventory into A, B, C categories. If this has not been accomplished, do it now. Our objective in this step is to sell off inventory in ASCENDING order of need. We are going to start with the inventory that is least used and move up to inventory that turns more frequently.

1. Get out your inventory study.
2. Call C inventory customers today and/or place ads to get rid of the C Class inventory immediately. Turn it into scrap if necessary. Take the write down on the books for any losses, but make all C inventory go away for cash...it does have carrying costs you don't need.
3. Start your inventory sales cash account
4. Continue on with Class B inventory. Make flyer's or lists and sell down class B inventory as Per Part 1 instructions. If you find a sales run on class B inventory, than pull back what you need, otherwise let it go.
5. Add any inventory sales revenue to your inventory cash account.
6. At this point you have cleaned up inventory to only what sells and/or what is needed to make sales. Adjust inventory levels to meet the new conditions of the marketplace.
7. From here forward, any inventory that does not turn quickly is reduced to cash (sold).
8. Do spot checks of all inventory for quantity, value and turns. I usually monitor ALL high value inventory daily...or weekly in some cases where the information, control systems and security is good.

Retail: I am going to talk about retail a bit here. In retail you are already familiar with closeouts and discounts. It's the same strategy, but I want you to recognize that most retailers tend to place too much value on items they buy for resale than pure inventory items used in making something. Retailers you need the cash now... because cash allows you to have options. It is essential you convert all slow moving inventory to cash as fast as you can.

Cash in the bank means you have options.

Final word on inventory sales: Sometimes your best customer for under-utilized inventory is the company that sold it to you in the first place. Even a sale back at a 25% restocking fee (a loss), is better than holding on to the inventory and folding the company. Sell it back. **Remember, add the cash to the cash reserves account.**

Phase 2, Step 11: Reduce Outstanding Debt Cash Flow

In this step we are going to ask for help from our creditors in several ways. We need the cooperation of our creditors if we are going to survive as they can have a big impact on our outflow of cash during the recovery period.

1 The premise of this step is "I need (your/some) help".

2 Get out your "debt detail" from Phase 1, Step 3.

3 I want you to determine the immediate cash per month you need to survive as a business. Put that monthly figure on the board or on a sheet of paper. Determine how much of that figure is divided between short and long term debt.

4 In each category (short and long term debt), I want you to evaluate your Debit detail and figure out two important classes of debt:

 4.1 Who is most willing to abandon or reduce the debt owed them

 4.2 Who is most willing to postpone payments for the debt owed them

5 For 4.1 creditors, I want you to write a brief form letter and send it to them by email addressed to the manager of the firm asking for a private conversation to discuss your current business condition. Do not go into any details, just ask for the meeting and say it is to "discuss your account". This gives them a heads up your not over there to buy more of anything. This is not a customer call for discussing more sales.

 5.1 You want to get the creditor to agree to abandon or reduce the debt owed them so meet with only the person who can wave off your debt, be it the manager, VP or CEO. Most creditors will have a policy regarding this and you need to know what that policy is and how firm that policy is.

 5.2 I am not saying every creditor will do this or even one...but I am saying that if you are honest and ask for a reduction, you might be surprised in what they are willing to do. At the least they might postpone the debt.

6 For 4.2 postponement creditors, I want you call each one on the phone personally and say something like the following:

 6.1 "Our company is undergoing financial restructuring with the goals of improving our cash flow and our payment certainty. Your debt is important to us. Our business is not in immediate trouble, but we are heading off a deeper crisis. We want you to receive every dime owed to you as we work out our recovery plan. That Plan uses a very rigid process, but for this effort to be successful, we need your help."

 6.2 "Can I count on your cooperation?" (They almost always say "yes".)

 6.3 "What we need is to postpone your next 3 payments from us. According to our new cash analysis, your next scheduled payment under our plan would be paid on ________________ and we are certain of this date. Would this be acceptable to you." *(Do not say a word until they respond fully to this statement. They are likely to clarify each point again so they have time to absorb your request).*

6.3.1 If they say yes, then hand deliver the payment or have it delivered exactly one business day earlier than they expected it.

6.3.2 If they say no, then ask them to reconsider and exit the phone conversation quickly after thanking them with something like the following statement.

6.3.2.1 ""We value your relationship and are confident in our recovery efforts. We are not abandoning your debt, but we could use your consideration of our current condition and recovery needs. We will keep you informed as conditions (change/improve). I am sorry you are not in a position to help us improve our financial conditions. Thank you for considering our needs and this relationship. If you change your mind, we would like to work out a solution". *(Now wait...no matter what...say nothing else...not a sound, just wait for a reply).*

6.3.2.2 Sometimes when people "try on a decision" they realize after second consideration that that decision does not "feel right" or that "the end result is not going to improve their sales relationship with your company". To deny your request is almost like saying "your business is not important to us".

6.3.2.2.1 Now for some companies who have no heart, your business might not matter. But for most this is not the case. All business is important no matter the size. We want them to extend some compassion and compassion only comes when a person understands the depth of your condition, your needs and can associate your conditions with a feeling of understanding.

6.3.2.2.2 On occasion, I have used the actual facts leading up to the financial condition "as a story" to help people understand what you have gone through and what you can do from here forward. For someone to have compassion, they truly need to feel what you are feeling...either from "being there before personally", or because they "feel what you feel". Tap into those powerful feelings.

7 For the people in 4.1, I want you to have the same conversation with each one, except this time I want it "face to face" in their office. Bring someone else from your office with you to show commitment if necessary.

8 This is not a time to have an ego so leave it behind. I have found that most people want to help other people. Sometimes their internal policies get in the way and sometimes they do not have the authority to say yes. The important thing here is to be "humble without cowering" and "polite without sucking up". This is just business and you need help and they are in a position to help.

9 I have handled multi-million dollar accounts in a "cordial manner". I know this process is effective...but a tough sell. Companies do help companies survive because the downside is "very down". Most creditors will do exactly as you request....but remember in the end, the person making the decision has to be the one who is in control of the decision...not you.

Grace and compassion come from the giver...just look at Jesus

Phase 2, Step 12: A,B, C, Assets Sales

In Part 1, we divided our fixed movable assets into three classes, A, B, and C. Here we are going to make cash fast by using a logical plan to sell off these assets in ascending order of least impact to the company.

I am going to take a small company approach here as larger companies have different assets and resources that can be treated quite differently including major auctions, obtaining loans, etc...but the same process would apply from a sales perspective. I am not minimizing the importance of large companies benefiting from the use of a formal asset classification system and priority sale process designed to sell off those unneeded items. Most lean companies are well beyond this step as proper asset management is efficient and measured.

Here we go...

- Advertise and sell off Class C assets for the highest price you can obtain, but sell them **within one week**. Take the cash and put into your cash reserve account. Do not touch this money under any circumstances. **This will be the last money you have.** Call it your "cash of last resort" fund. This money should be separate from the cash raised in inventory sales.
- Advertise all Class B items in free listings (such as www.craigslist.org). Make a good description on the item, take good quality photos and set a reasonable price on these items. Don't expect highest dollar for anything being sold. **You want the cash, not the item.** Add this revenue to your "cash of last resort" account. Photos and good descriptions sell.

  Sell off Class B and C as soon as you can so you can stay in business.
- Class A items require some careful thought and some frank consideration of what will be left after the sale. Take the complete ABC list and sort the A items according to what cash they bring into the company per month or per year. If you don't know this information then "guesstimate" for each one, but honestly you or your Production Foreman should know this information almost off hand. You will will want to sell off these assets from the bottom up of the A-asset class. Anything that contributes less than 5% is sold first, 10% second and so on. This way you are selling off least important A-assets to most important.
  - If you get to 30% items, your going to be looking at a completely different company. Let's look at this point as it relates to wealth:

There is a huge difference between asset recovery to improve cash on hand and selling off business wealth. Once you start selling off Class A assets, you are either going out of business, or are heavily modifying your business model and offerings to the market.

Phase 2, Step 13: Overhead and Expense Account Reduction

In step Phase 1, Step #5, we look hard at overhead and expenses. We understood issues like:

1. Where are the major outflows going?
2. How is the overhead tied to revenue?
3. What is the ranking of overhead in terms of outflow dollars per period?
4. What overhead is sensitive to revenue and what is not?
5. What correlation exists between expense accounts and revenue?

Combined, these studies provided a much needed look into the world of overhead and expense accounts. By now, you should have a good feel for what needs to be reduced and where. This can include decisions on where the company is located, how much overhead is needed to maintain a reduced revenue, and so on.

It's time to trim some fat. Here is my list of how that can be done and why.

1 In a cash crisis the need for sustaining overhead and expense accounts at previous levels is just plain ludicrous. The company is running out of money and as we know, money (cash) is the "life blood" of the business.

2 Staff will need to do more with far less if you are going to get control of the outflow. The cash budgeting and cash allocation processes proposed in prior steps will go a long way towards reducing and monitoring outflow until such time as the company is making sustained net positive cash, has built a reserve and is increasing it's sales.

3 We are going to cover RIF in a later Step, so let's pass on the "human side" of the overhead equation.

4 What we want to do here is bring the whole level down...way down, until "everyone is squealing". By that, I mean that every department is talking to the core team about what they are doing without and how much it is needed. Here, I need to make a distinction between "what is needed to do their jobs" and "what is just a nuisance absence". I am talking only about stopping "nuisance items". At that point, reduction in overhead is about right. No one group or entity should be "business as usual" while other internal groups "can't even buy pencils". Everyone should be making a sacrifice. This includes Management and Sales departments who tend to spend more than others...employee for employee.

5 As a starting point lower overhead 10% across the board. Then go to 15% and then 20%. At 30% you either had way too much overhead to begin with, or the company will fold from deeper reasons than just having excess overhead.

6 Let's look at our list again from the prior step for guidance on what can be done and when.

6.1 **Indirect labor:** Apply the percentages

6.2 **Labor benefits:** Everything you are not obligated to provide needs to stop

6.3 **Retirement:** No change...they earned it...watch for escalating perks.

6.4 **Management incentives:** This is a big one. The incentives could cover a wide list. Here is my take on the issue.

6.4.1 Management does not deserve incentives if the company is failing...period. The incentive now is to keep your job and not be fired for miss-management of company resources, failing to bring about fiscal performance, or both.

6.4.2 Management needs to lead by example and all those perks of being at the top needs to be given up....at least temporarily. Once the company is on its feet again and 6 months of outflow is in the bank, then you can talk about incentives.

6.4.3 I'll bet nine out of ten Senior Managers will not give up anything of significance.

6.5 **Supplies:** Just cut back heavily to "must haves".

6.6 **Taxes:** Not much to do here, but it is worth speaking with a tax advisor to make sure you cannot obtain a tax relief or an advantage in some way during the crisis...taking a loss included.

6.7 **Insurance:** Big issue for most people. Property, all risk, loss of income and liability policies need to be looked at. Consider filing for loss of income if the policy includes this clause. Ask your underwriter what can be done to reduce premiums.

6.8 **Rentals:** Some should go away, some should be added if the Plan is being overseen correctly. Recall, we said we were going to sell some "low use" items and rent them back as needed?

6.9 **Depreciation:** You already have a loss and accelerated depreciation will not help this cause.

6.10 **Utilities:** Get frugal. Turn off all non-essential lights, equipment, computers, machinery, etc.

6.11 **Telephone/Internet:** Pick up all "non-critical" cell phones and cancel the service. The hit now is far less than the expense of leaving them in place for a bill later. Go to a system where all "out of area calls" will be made using the Internet. There are companies out there who specialize in "Voice Over Internet Protocol (VOIP).

6.12 **Travel:** What travel? Unless the travel is to close a large deal, it is not necessary and when it is it should be very frugal.

6.13 **Outside Services:** I covered this in Phase 1, Step #5 and in Part 1. Services will be reduced to the least possible.

6.14 **Entertainment:** This is a "like to do" issue and should already be reduced if not eliminated so not a consideration here.

6.15 **Dues and Donations:** All non-essential dues are canceled. Donations will just have to wait because you might be the one needing the donation.

6.16 **Advertising:** Covered in prior step and in Part 1 under "Advertising". Roll it back, defer it, anything to conserve cash.

6.17 **Sales Commissions:** I am going to address this more here as it can lead to good savings and higher returns.

6.17.1 Move every outside salesman to a reduced commission structure. I like 50% pay, 50% commissions. If they baulk, then they are not producers. Make sure you up the commissions to compensate for the change.

Well there you go. If you do everything above, you have likely made a significant dent in cash outflow from overhead and expense accounts. Expense Accounts was covered in both Part 1 and in Phase 1, Step 5 so no further action here unless you have not done it.

Outflows that must be managed

Payroll and Payroll Taxes
Inventory
Rent (cash out)
Leases
Utilities
Phone
Marketing/Sales
Administration
Insurance
Professional
Other Operating
Corporate Taxes
Retirement Payments
Interest Payments
Debt Payments
Other Payments

Phase 2, Step 14: Labor Reduction

Labor reduction is a "double edged sword". On one edge you convert labor to dollars. On the other edge, "excess labor" reduces profitability. Labor is not automatically synchronized, where an increase in labor means a corresponding increase in revenues. Here the core team and line managers can provide the necessary input of who needs to stay, and who needs to go. Let's look at a method and some advice.

1 Do not call everyone together and let them know that a RIF is being planned. This will only cause drama and people will change their behavior. Good people will start looking for a new job and bad people will "milk the work" they have.

2 Instead call the core team together and discuss the labor issue with them. By now, because we studied this in Phase 1, you should have a good feeling of how much labor is needed to meet the current revenue. Likely it is less than you now have if you are honest.

  2.1 I evaluate people for RIF by "skills" and not head count. If you understand what skills are needed to do the level of business you have, then the only question is "how can I obtain those skills for the least amount of money". That sounds good in theory, but it is not the whole story... consider "seniority".

    2.1.1 Seniority is a big issue. I think that seniority has an influence in the equation of whether to keep someone of not, but it is not the only deciding factors. I like to use a "30/30/30/10" formula. While not perfect...it seems to work well in practice.

      2.1.1.1 30% is skills...fairly black and white.

      2.1.1.2 30% is performance, attendance, dedication, etc. You can break it down anyway you want to what is important.

      2.1.1.3 30% is seniority. The more seniority, the more weight it should have, but it is not the deciding factor only.

      2.1.1.4 and 10% is "management discretion". This last 10% is reserved so line or senior management can have some level of control over the outcome in a tie situation. It is not all about "mechanical people performing some mechanical task". It is also about human relationships and the ability to work together. Management can swing a tie to the one they most want to work with going forward.

3 I am going to say the following statement very frankly. "Anyone not on board with the recovery is gone...today...this hour". Write them their check. There is no time to negotiate a motivated solution and save a poison condition. Best to wave goodbye and show the troops you mean business.

4 Bring the company down in stages, not all at once.

5 Consider having them come back on as sub-contractors or as consultants on an "as needed basis". You never know things might pick up...maybe in a few days.

My last thought is to choose RIF carefully. You are dealing with peoples lives and a major part of every company...its people.

I have found for the most part it is painfully obvious to those people who consider themselves as non-essential employees. If you must fire someone, do it in the morning, behind closed doors and allow them time to recover emotionally and speak their mind before sending in the next RIF target. You will learn more in that conversation than you have all year poking and prodding. Ask them specifically what they feel is wrong with the company. They may know of a log jamb your not aware of. Do it with love and try if possible to help them smoothly move forward. Let the ones left behind know they are safe as soon as possible.

Cash Flow Position	(Bold = Actual. Std. = Planned)	Example	Day 1	Day 2
Cash In	Cash Sales	100.00		
Cash In	Credit Sales	100.00		
Cash In	Interest	100.00		
Cash In	Rentals	100.00		
Cash In	Billed Sales	100.00		
Cash In	Project 1	100.00		
Cash In	Project 2	100.00		
Cash In	Project 3	100.00		
Cash In	Progress Payments	100.00		
Cash In	Customer Advances	100.00		
Cash In	Interest on Loans	100.00		
Cash In	Rent or Rental Payments (cash In)	100.00		
Cash In	Cash Sales	100.00		
Cash In	Other Receipts	100.00		
	Total Income	**1400.00**	**0.00**	**0.00**
Cash Out	Payroll and Payroll Taxes	100.00		
Cash Out	Inventory	100.00		
Cash Out	Rent (cash out)	100.00		
Cash Out	Leases	100.00		
Cash Out	Utilities	100.00		
Cash Out	Phone	100.00		
Cash Out	Marketing/Sales	100.00		
Cash Out	Administration	100.00		
Cash Out	Insurance	100.00		
Cash Out	Professional	100.00		
Cash Out	Other Operating	100.00		
Cash Out	Corporate Taxes	100.00		
Cash Out	Retirement Payments	100.00		
Cash Out	Interest Payments	100.00		
Cash Out	Debt Payments	100.00		
Cash Out	Other Payments	100.00		
	Total Payments	**1600.00**	**0.00**	**0.00**
	Net Cash Flow	**-200.00**	**0.00**	**0.00**
	Starting Cash Position	**200.00**	**0.00**	**0.00**
	Ending Cash Position	**0.00**	**0.00**	**0.00**

Phase 3, Step 15: Cash allocation and budgeting in accordance with known budgets and priorities (customer, project or business unit)

Here is where "the rubber meets the road", so to speak. Everything up to this point was designed to help you fill in this form with a high degree of confidence and knowledge.

Basically you should know by now:

1 What you sold by time

2 How sales are tied into expenses such as:

 2.1 How direct and indirect expenses are tied to sales

   2.2 How inventory factors into making money
   2.3 How much inventory you need to make money
3 Income projections by project or business unit
4 Planned cash needs over time by project or business unit
5 Fixed cash needs over time by project or business unit
6 Summaries of cash outflow projections noting when events should occur
7 Your present and current cash position

Here we go....

You accomplish this task by placing information into a similar spreadsheet you create such as the basic Cash Flow Position sheet shown above. Each of the categories in the sample shown needs to be "fleshed out" with hard numbers, or estimated as best possible. This can be accomplished by either the Leader, your accountant, bookkeeper, or all three.

It should include firm hard commitments and estimates of cash outflow and inflow when firm commitments are not yet known. Use a roll-up type system so you can, at a glance, know **firm commitments** (outstanding P.O's we will keep, lease payments, insurance, etc.) and "soft numbers" meaning **estimates** (projections, assumptions or "rules of thumb"). Anything to get the best possible numbers into the form. I use a computerized spreadsheet and typically include a combination of columns and bold numbers to accomplish this notation, but alternatively, you could also use the "notes feature" for active cells. Some times I have just used a "comments field" in a more manual system. Anything so you know what is real and what is estimated numbers.

Most businesses have a good idea what cash they absolutely need this week. That **certainty** decreases for some numbers as the time horizon extends into the future. If you can't predict with certainty this week's expenses, then there likely is a deeper problem needing to be addressed. It might be time to get back to the basics of management "by the numbers" until you do know cost with certainty.

Some items will be firm commitments planned out over a fixed, long, time horizon...like lease payments, etc. Some values will be estimates on Day 1, like "What I am going to spend for office supplies...(don't laugh...when times get really tough you should be counting all smaller purchase amounts). The key is to make these values the best possible. **Fill out your form as best possible. It will be needed in the main Cash Position Spreadsheet.**

Net Cash Flow, Starting Cash Position, and Ending Cash Position are the bottom line to how we are doing.

Phase 3, Step 16: Applying the work "real time"

Let's recap so we can build on the work accomplished to achieve our final goal of "real time cash management" from a cash crisis event.

In **Phase 0,** we assembled the team and created a sense of urgency
In **Phase 1, Step 1,** we prepared an "Income History"
In **Phase 1, Step 2,** we analyzed inventory and purchase patterns
In **Phase 1, Step 3,** we looked at Debt in detail and summarized all debts
In **Phase 1, Step 4,** we reviewed Labor
In **Phase 1, Step 5,** we took a hard look at Overhead
In **Phase 1, Step 6,** we considered opportunities for Direct Expense reduction
In **Phase 1, Step 7,** we analyzed individual expense account relationships to sales
In **Phase 2, Step 8,** we prepared an "Income Projection" using a "Sales Forecast"
In **Phase 2, Step 9,** we forecast cash outflow by project or business unit
In **Phase 2, Step 10,** we made efforts to turn slow inventory into cash
In **Phase 2, Step 11,** we made efforts to reduce or postpone outstanding debt
In **Phase 2, Step 12,** we made efforts to turn underutilized and unneeded assets into cash
In **Phase 2, Step 13,** we reduced overhead and expense accounts
In **Phase 2, Step 14,** we handled a reduction in labor
In **Phase 3, Step 15,** we allocated cash in accordance with known budgets and priorities
Phase 3, Step 16, we will apply the work of cash management in "real time"

I have do doubt that Steps 1-15 represented quite a lot of work for most companies. Now it is time to put all that work into practice in Step 16 by applying the information "real time." Let's set the stage using our "Cash Flow Position" form. Please refer to it.

Presently, we have:

- Completely filled out the Cash Flow Position form with our best information
- A starting cash position
- Planned cash receipts for the day, week and month and beyond
- Defined our expenses for the day, week and month and beyond
- Established a provision to know which numbers are "planned" and which ones are "actual". **Hint**: I either use two distinct number columns or **bold** actual numbers

Cash Flow Position	(Bold = Actual, Std = Planned)	Example	Day 1	Day 2
Cash In	Cash Sales	100.00		
Cash In	Credit Sales	100.00		
Cash In	Interest	100.00		
Cash In	Rentals	100.00		
Cash In	Billed Sales	100.00		
Cash In	Project 1	100.00		
Cash In	Project 2	100.00		
Cash In	Project 3	100.00		
Cash In	Progress Payments	100.00		
Cash In	Customer Advances	100.00		
Cash In	Interest on Loans	100.00		
Cash In	Rent or Rental Payments (cash In)	100.00		
Cash In	Cash Sales	100.00		
Cash In	Other Receipts	100.00		
	Total Income	**1400.00**	**0.00**	**0.00**
Cash Out	Payroll and Payroll Taxes	100.00		
Cash Out	Inventory	100.00		
Cash Out	Rent (cash out)	100.00		
Cash Out	Leases	100.00		
Cash Out	Utilities	100.00		
Cash Out	Phone	100.00		
Cash Out	Marketing/Sales	100.00		
Cash Out	Administration	100.00		
Cash Out	Insurance	100.00		
Cash Out	Professional	100.00		
Cash Out	Other Operating	100.00		
Cash Out	Corporate Taxes	100.00		
Cash Out	Retirement Payments	100.00		
Cash Out	Interest Payments	100.00		
Cash Out	Debt Payments	100.00		
Cash Out	Other Payments	100.00		
	Total Payments	**1600.00**	**0.00**	**0.00**
	Net Cash Flow	**-200.00**	**0.00**	**0.00**
	Starting Cash Position	**200.00**	**0.00**	**0.00**
	Ending Cash Position	**0.00**	**0.00**	**0.00**

Using the cash position spreadsheet:

1. We start on Day 1 and make sure "what we plan is exactly what happens".
2. We ensure the income planned for the week is certain.
3. We monitor our income horizon with 100% dedication.
4. We approve all expenses for the day and review planned expenses for the week to income planned. Any short fall will require new cash or postponement of the expense.

5. We work though any problems that develop so we remain certain of our income and our outflows to the penny.
6. We check the main numbers of Net Cash Flow, Starting Cash and Ending Cash for issues and trends.

Analyzing the Cash Position spreadsheet:

Let's analyze the main numbers in the Cash Flow Position Spreadsheet: (parentheses show possible directions for the values and their possible impact).

- **Net Cash Flow (Positive and/or rising compared to previous time cycle):** This is the desirable condition. We want our net cash flow to be positive and increasing as it shows we are building cash into our financial system. The more cash we build into the system the more we can pay for our business survival and growth. It's that simple.
- **Net Cash Flow (Negative and/or falling compared to previous time cycle):** Not a desirable condition. It says we need to make serious adjustments to our sales income and our outflows. Either we need to sell more, or we need to cut expenses to achieve a positive net cash flow position. ***This is critical. You must achieve a positive Net Cash Position at all cost and the sooner the better.*** Large companies with heavy reserves can afford to loose money (state negative earnings) for perhaps years. You can't....this takes away from your starting cash position on the next time cycle. It makes your starting cash position less in value by the exact amount your ending cash is negative.
- **Starting Cash Position (Rising compared to previous time cycle):** This is the desirable condition. We want to have more money in our financial system, not less. If each time cycle our starting cash position is increasing, we are doing something right. Normally that means we are controlling our outflows and/or increasing our inflows.
- **Starting Cash Position (Falling compared to previous time cycle):** Not a desirable condition. A falling cash position means we are losing money compared to the previous time cycle. Get the reins of the company here. We need an increasing cash position each time cycle if at all possible. At first it might be all negative. Then as you get a handle on things this should reverse to all positive. If you have negative net cash flow and no money in starting position, then either outside money needs to be put in, or, the outflows need to be postponed until the money is available. There are no other options.
- **Ending Cash Position (Rising compared to previous time cycle):** We are making money and increasing our starting position of cash for the next time cycle. **This is the single most important barometer of how we are doing. If we are making cash, then it will not only be positive...it will be rising in value over time.**
- **Ending Cash Position (Falling compared to previous time cycle):** If it is declining, then we have an expense or a condition we need to acknowledge or change immediately. When this value goes to zero or negative, someone

is going to have to kick in money and pay for the loss....usually the owner of the business.

Recovery depends on your ability to read these numbers and increase cash on hand and ultimately make reserves.

Fluctuations in the end numbers and some key questions to ask

Let's discuss "cycle-to-cycle fluctuations" in your numbers. When you compare one time cycle to another, item for item, look behind the numbers to the sources for the change. If Starting Cash is declining, then look at Net Cash components of previous cycles to find the answer. Either income declined or outflow increased in the previous cycle. Once we find the principal indicators for the change in numbers, (cycle time to cycle time), we need to ask ourselves a number of questions that lead to answers you can act on:

Assess

- ☐ Why did the change in numbers occur?
- ☐ Is the problem escalating, stable or reducing?
- ☐ Am I looking at a symptom or a systemic problem?
- ☐ What do my people know about this issue and its cause?
- ☐ Who is in charge of this issue?
- ☐ Can I go behind the numbers and physically touch and see what makes up the numbers?
- ☐ What processes are we using and did it cause this condition?
- ☐ What triggered this issue to occur?
- ☐ What help can I bring in to solve this problem?
- ☐ Have I got a clear understanding of the problem statement?
- ☐ Is there a security issue here, like theft?
- ☐ What will happen if this impact hits again in the next time cycle?

Reduce Impact

- ☐ Can I come up with something "out of the box", right now, today, that will cause this condition not to occur?
- ☐ If it is going to happen, is there something I can do right now to lessen the impact?
- ☐ Who do I need to inform about the issue?
- ☐ Who is best suited to solve this problem?

Intermediate steps

- ☐ What is our intermediate goal for this?
- ☐ What additional resources are needed to solve the problem?
- ☐ Do we have a list of possible solutions?

- ☐ Is there something I can do to stop it from happening again in the next time cycle?
- ☐ How can we monitor this issue short term so we can see what is making it change?

Long term steps

- ☐ What is our long term goal for this?
- ☐ Is there a way to modify the process so the root cause making this condition is eliminated for good?
- ☐ How do we monitor the condition long term?

When we look at cash flow in minute detail, (across days or even weeks), we are going to see variations, (and even negative values), for Net Cash. This could be because we had a lease payment due that we paid, or we had a tax payment due we paid. These fluctuations, (while they sometimes look awful), are normal during recovery and beyond.

Sometimes changes in outflow hits the cash side of the business....but not always. Sometimes we close up a project, or we stop selling something seasonal. This loss of income in these situations can either be temporary or permanent. If we lose a steady repeat customer, then our income base declines - so for that case it is permanent until the revenue is replaced.

Let's look at the chart of numbers for a fictitious business as an example.

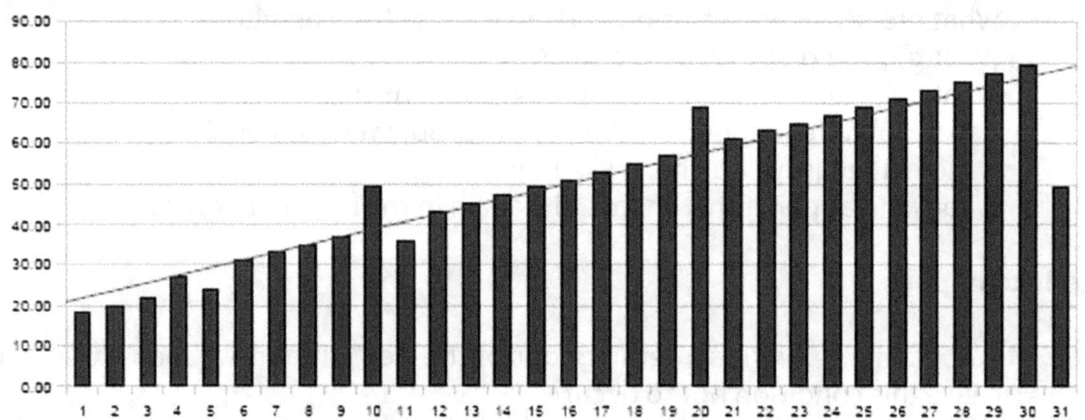

Above, I created this simple picture of NET CASH FLOW over 31 days to show that on Day 10 and day 20, we had some additional income. On Day 5, 11 and 31 we paid out routine expenses that showed up as a declining net cash flow for those days. However, the overall cash flow trend is positive and even with a typical monthly outflow at the end of the time cycle month series we look positive and good. Now let's look at what happens to the ending cash position as this is the most important.

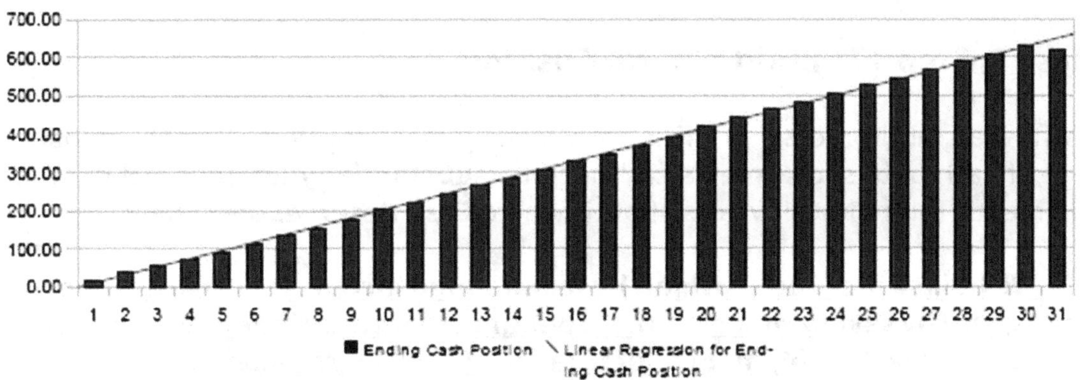

It is hard to see, but can you find above a fall in ENDING CASH POSITION on day 31 when we made our end of the month payments?

On Day 31 we had a *negative* NET CASH FLOW value. It reduced our Ending Cash Position, but that outflow was expected and needed...therefore it is acceptable and the end result is that overall our month end cash position is increasing.

Negative End Cash Projection: Now, had the negative end cash position continued to decline, we would eat away at our Starting Cash Position to the point where we would have to either put money in to sustain the business while we figured out what was wrong, or close the business and file as bankrupt.

All these relationships are important. We must be able to relate how our business is functioning and confirm our projected cash position with absolute certainty. You cannot pay bills with "profit" or "negative ending cash positions".

Daily Work on the Cash Flow Position and Supporting Documents

A high degree of daily discipline is needed to keep these forms up to date. **It is essential that you keep the Cash Flow Position Spreadsheet and all supporting documents up to date each work day, <u>without exception</u>.** Get behind a few days and the information is stale and the cash position becomes uncertain or unstable. The value of keeping this work up to date is that at a moments notice you know where you are cash wise, what you can spend and when.

Easy to maintain...hard to bring current. You know this because you are now current and understand the effort involved...right?

Every time there is a change in outflow or income, you must make a proper correction in the forms to reflect that change.

<u>**Each person should do their very best to limit the use of funds to only what is absolutely essential for the continuance of the operation and the projects under the control of the business.**</u>

Phase 3, Step 17: Build a "Cash Cushion"

The Plan (and process) of Crisis Cash Management supports internal management of cash until such time as cash income **substantially leads** actual cash requirements. This net positive cash flow is where **Cash Reserves** are created.

We build a nice cash cushion by maintaining income far in excess of expenses, and by saving that cash (not spending it) until sufficient to weather at least six (6) months of total loss of business income.

We can only spend the money in excess of the 6 month reserve.

The above implies that our initial target goal is to build a reserve equal to six (6) months of expenses WITHOUT ANY INCOME. In practice, a 100% loss for each month would not normally occur...even in a marginally performing business as any income received would offset some of the losses sustained. However, it does not diminish the intent of the goal which is to build a tidy reserve you can bank on.

Start small with a small goal of one week's expenses. Then move to one month's expenses and so on, until 6 or more months of reserves are achieved. You would be delighted how good it feels to have 6 month's reserves in the bank. Few smaller companies can actually say that.

This is not a fund for expansion, nor is it a "let's go buy that new laser cutting table" fund. It is a "cushion fund" designed to provide you with a means to weather almost any situation. Sure, unplanned expenses are naturally going to occur and according to "Murphy's Law" usually they happen at the worst possible time. The cash cushion you are creating allows for unplanned expenses to occur without it being a "death sentence" or major drama of finding the needed money to cover the unplanned expense.

Liquid cash always allows for options.

Here in reserve cash is where your recovery is felt most. It is a welcome day when you can see the results of your efforts in the form of making unpressed business decisions how best to invest your excess cash.

Now, go build those reserves and celebrate.

Phase 3, Step 18: Celebrate the wins

I covered this in Part 1 fairly well, but after all you have accomplished, it is a good reminder as you work to celebrate your wins...both large and small. I can see that some of you more frugal managers might need some "milestones" to celebrate over so here goes.

Milestones

We are getting down to the end, so we need some final milestones to allow us to monitor our progress and know when we have accomplished the important tasks. Just like a progress report or road map, we need to know when we have moved towards positive cash flow as major achievements. Hopefully this helps you get in the mood to celebrate.

Milestones of Crisis Cash Management (in ascending order):

1. You understand what Crisis Cash Flow Management is and how to achieve it
2. You have built a team with a sense of urgency
3. You have stopped all but necessary spending
4. You have sold off underutilized inventory
5. You have sold off unneeded assets
6. You have created a cash reserve account for the final push if things go really bad
7. You have developed your information collection system including forms and data sources.
8. Everyone knows their job and is formally committed to contribute to the recovery
9. Information vehicles are now populated
10. All money in and out of the business flows through the Crisis Cash Management System
11. You have achieved your first positive net cash flow day
12. You have a growing end cash position, cycle to cycle
13. You have created cash reserves equal to:
    a) one weeks expense (average of all monthly expense)
    b) one month
    c) 3 months
    d) 6 months
    e) 1 year
    f) 2 years

Use the milestones above as a means to celebrate your wins...small and large. I consider each one a major step in your recovery.

Recognition:

(This is brief for the reason that no amount of words will motivate someone to reward others...it must come from the heart and it must come in the form of actions.)

Nothing does more for the spirit of the employee, (or those stakeholders who supported your efforts), than recognition for a "job well done". If you feel this way then say so in six basic ways:

1. Tell them individually
2. Show them individually
3. Tell them collectively
4. Show them collectively
5. Highlight those who stood out in front of others so they can see what a leader looks like
6. Show them with real and grateful hard evidence of your gratitude.
    1. For banks that is **growing your business**.
    2. For suppliers that would be **more orders**.
    3. For employees that would be **unanticipated tax free cash**.

Closing Thoughts:

I'm not going to say reaching positive cash flow and real time cash management will be easy, nor impossible for a declining business. I will say that the rewards are great and risk of business closure decrease as cash risk decreases.

As I close out this work of joy, I want to leave you with a few key "first day of recovery thoughts" based on my experience and beliefs:

1. I will honor God by giving back to him his due portion of all my earnings
2. I will believe I can reverse a declining cash position when the numbers and conditions say I can
3. I will spend no cash unless the expense quickly makes more cash than I am spending
4. I understand there is nothing to manage without sales and cash income
5. I will know the difference between my internal business failure and an external business cycle decline
6. I will plan my cash flow position each day and keep my cash flow information current each and every day
7. All the bills of my business will be paid on time and with cleared funds...not paid by credit or by floating the check
8. I will work with my suppliers and my creditors to find the best recovery solution
9. I will understand that profits are not cash
10. I will sell off any obsolete inventory or inventory I don't need
11. I will empower people and hold them accountable for their performance

12. I will not "pull the plug" on my declining business too late
13. I will involve my external stakeholders in all cash recovery plans that involve them
14. I will celebrate small and large wins as we progress in recovery
15. I will make the process enjoyable...not a "life sentence"
16. I will treat everyone with respect and ask for their help for I am not too proud to say I need their help
17. I will reward those who made our recovery possible in as many ways as I can

The Future: Rising Business Taxes:

From several perspectives, I fear that most U.S. businesses are about to get hammered by the proposed changes in the U.S. Tax Code. These include:

1. *Loss of revenue from a declining business sales tax*
2. *Carbon Tax on cabon usage and emmissions*
3. *Aging baby boomer healthcare deficit*
4. *Growing national debt*
5. *Decline in the value of the dollar*

Make sure you understand these tax law changes and work to modify the company to suit what is in the best interest of the firm. I know of some companies, (mine included), who are investigating ways to shift their entire enterprise business model to react to these potential tax code changes. Consult your tax attorney and accountant for affective stratiges.

Reversing Bad Management and Changing Bad Business Models:

While there's a lot of advice throughout this Guide and Plan, simply applying the advice cannot fix a poorly performing business suffering from external causes, bad management, or a poor business model and value proposition. It's up to YOU to make the necessary changes in your business to ACCESS, RECOVER, MINIMIZE CONSEQUENCE and PREVENT if possible, the conditions that got created this crisis in the first place.

Here is the best advice in the book.

Normally, recovery means finding and applying EXTERNAL SUPPORT from a competent consulting firm...including my own. No, I am not making a sales pitch. Instead, I want you to understand that I care about people and their goals. After 25 years of being on the front lines, I have learned that most CEO's and Senior Managers are just too close to the situation to see the business in a pure unbiased business light, nor do most companies have people standing around who can study the business, (and have the skills needed). Nor is time available to re-engineer a new business model, let alone support the changes needed to bring a new model about. Please, please, find someone you can trust and above all be open, honest and ready to receive new ideas. Many I fear will let their ego and need for control get in the way of positive business change and success through the cooperation of others. Be that open and resourceful business owner who is a delight to work with.

Thank you for taking the time to read this humble work. I hope this book provided you with at least one idea or concept which caused you to think, do, or act differently. If it did I consider the book a success. Please tell others if you liked what you read.

Ask God for his blessing. Luck has nothing to do with your recovery.

All the best,

Jim Rohr

ABOUT THE AUTHOR

Jim Rohr *has led several businesses, provided turn around coaching, best practice, market analysis, business and financial consulting support to leading companies, government agencies and start-ups for over 25 years. Jim has managed over one billion in spend for a large multinational and Chaired an "industry wide" Panel on Business Process Technology.*

Jim is a motivational leader and has participated or overseen initiatives such as Business Analysis, ERP Selection and Implementation, Management Information Systems, Strategic Sourcing, Balanced Score Card, AP/AR Analysis, Strategic Management, Risk Management, Business Model Origination/Modification and Enterprise Wide Change Management Initiatives. His current work involves developing fundamental business models for new businesses and refinement of existing business models for firms needing specialized business coaching.

Jim is a published author and contributor to several enterprises. Today, Jim is semi-retired and works for select Companies and Governments who need special help in achieving critical strategic goals. He is currently writing an extensive book on Sales titled "The 10 Reasons Why Buyers Don't Buy". Look for it in stores soon.

Contact

If you would like to contact Jim Rohr you can send him an email to:

jimships@yahoo.com

www.ingramcontent.com/pod-product-compliance
Lightning Source LLC
Chambersburg PA
CBHW081134170526
45165CB00008B/2669

* 9 7 8 1 4 3 9 2 6 2 5 2 8 *